NO EXPERIENCE NECESSARY

NO EXPERIENCE NECESSARY

Fulfilling the Gospel Commission Is Easier Than You Think

KARL HAFFNER

Nampa, Idaho | Oshawa, Ontario, Canada
www.pacificpress.com

Cover design by Gerald Lee Monks
Cover design resources from istockphoto.com/fotostorm, istockphoto.com/Dutko
Inside design by Aaron Troia

Additional copies of this book are available by calling toll-free 1-800-765-6955 or by visiting AdventistBookCenter.com.

Library of Congress Cataloging-in-Publication Data
Names: Haffner, Karl, 1961- author.
Title: No experience necessary : fulfilling the Gospel commission is easier than you think / Karl Haffner.
Description: Nampa : Pacific Press Publishing Association, 2018.
Identifiers: LCCN 2017056206 | ISBN 9780816363698 (pbk.)
Subjects: LCSH: Witness bearing (Christianity)—Biblical teaching.
Classification: LCC BV4520 .H34 2018 | DDC 248/.5—dc23 LC record available at https://lccn.loc.gov/2017056206

December 2017

DEDICATION

To Wayne and Hazel Burns

You are a great inspiration to me by how you show and share Jesus. Thank you for being a beautiful portrait of what it looks like to fulfill the every-day commission. It is a privilege to serve Jesus with you.

CONTENTS

PREFACE

When it comes to spiritual gifts, the gift of "evangelism" would definitely be ninth on my list . . . or maybe twenty-fifth—depending on which list you want to use. Ron Phillips tells me, "Most Christians are familiar with the nine gifts of the Spirit that Paul describes in 1 Corinthians 12:4-10. But did you know there are many more? Though the exact number is debatable, [there] are at least 25 spiritual gifts the Holy Spirit gave to the early church—and continues to give today."[1] However you figure, evangelism ranks at the bottom for me.

And I'm a pastor!

Yup, I've carried a lot of guilt over this. After all, if you're not winning souls for Jesus, then you're not a legit Jesus follower, right?

In his book *Evangelism for the Rest of Us*, Mike Bechtle reminds me that I'm not the only Christian who has struggled with this. Here's his story:

> I heard at least a hundred sermons on the Great Commission and our responsibility to carry it out. I even considered foreign missions at one point after hearing missionaries share stories about people coming to Christ like overripe fruit falling from a tree.
>
> I knew the verses about the fields being "white unto harvest" and heard guest speakers telling us to pray for laborers—then to be willing to go ourselves. I also had heard the passages about what would

> happen if I didn't share with someone: their blood would be on my head, meaning I would be responsible for those who died in their sins if I didn't share with them. I wasn't sure what that meant; I just knew I would be in trouble.
>
> I attended a small evangelical Bible college. Once each semester, classes were canceled and we attended a mandatory "day of visitation." We were each paired with a partner and then assigned to an evangelistic team for the morning—the mall team, the door-to-door team, the skid row team, and so forth. I dreaded those days and even managed to find myself ill a few times—too sick to participate. On the days I did participate, I tried to get on the skid row team. Somehow, sharing my faith felt less threatening when I could do it with a homeless person who was obviously needy. After a couple of hours, we returned to campus and shared stories about what had happened. Occasionally, someone actually reported praying with someone to receive Christ. I wondered why those stories never happened to me.[2]

Ditto. I've done the door-to-door days with disastrous results. I've preached the sermons and shamed the sheep for not being more intentional about "seeking the lost." All the while, I've struggled with this gaping gap in my own ministry. While my churches have experienced modest growth over the years, it's a far cry from what was happening in Pastor Peter's church: "Then those who accepted what Peter said were baptized. On that day about 3000 people were added to the group of believers" (Acts 2:41, ERV).

I wish that was my testimony. Perhaps it would be if only I were a better Bible-thumpin' evangelist, right? Or is my guilt misguided? Might God even use a coward like me to build His kingdom—even though evangelism barely registers on my spiritual gifts inventory? Can I still play a part in God's grand narrative of redeeming the lost human race?

Yes. Absolutely! And I don't need a spiritual gifts makeover first.

God can use me, and you, and every evangelistic misfit out there to carry out His mandate: "Therefore go and make disciples of all nations, baptizing them in the name of the Father and of the Son and of the Holy Spirit, and teaching them to obey everything I have commanded you. And surely I am with you always, to the very end of the age" (Matthew

28:19, 20). Take heart, fellow fraidy-cat; Jesus is with us in this journey!

So come on board. Let's explore Scripture and discover how God has uniquely gifted every one of us to accomplish what matters most to Him—reaching His kids for the kingdom. First, let's consider the questions that often derail evangelism; then we will look at the role models who show us how to be effective witnesses regardless of spiritual gifts; and finally, we'll consider the teaching of Jesus Himself on the subject of sharing Him.

Please don't feel intimidated by the invitation. I'm not asking you to go knock on doors. I'm only asking that we allow God to show us in His Word that it was never His intent to relegate evangelism to a few professionals who own pricey projectors. Sharing the good news is the privilege we all have. We can use our unique gifts, talents, and resources to change the world in Jesus' name. So for God's sake, let's go!

---

1. Ron Phillips, "25 Gifts of the Holy Spirit," *Charisma Magazine*, May 5, 2013, https://www.charismamag.com/spirit/supernatural/17428-the-gift-list.
2. Mike Bechtle, *Evangelism for the Rest of Us: Sharing Christ Within Your Personality Style* (Grand Rapids, MI: Baker Books, 2006), 14, 15.

SOME PEOPLE I APPRECIATE . . .

The exceptional team of pastors at the Kettering Church—your spirit makes the office feel like Kings Island.

Gary Burns—the encourager who is the whole reason for this book.

Jayne Bryant and Kathy Plowman—people who live their passion to share the gospel with others.

George Lewis—my golfing buddy who graciously loaned me his condo for a sabbatical to write this book.

Dave and Jill Evans—treasured friends whose dedication to the church is a thing of beauty.

Fred and Mary Kaye Manchur—models of putting God first, family second, and work third.

Wally and Julie Sackett—leaders who live and love like Jesus.

Ron Halvorsen and Oswaldo Magaña—boys who belong in the Best Bosses Hall of Fame.

Cherié, Lindsey, and Claire—the greatest people on the planet.

PROBLEMS

Any church that is not seriously involved
in helping fulfill the Great Commission
has forfeited its biblical right to exist.
—Oswald J. Smith

"Go into all the world and preach
the gospel to all creation."
—Jesus, Mark 16:15

Every Christian . . . is either
a missionary or an impostor.
—Charles Spurgeon

Chapter 1

ARE WE JUST TALKING TO OURSELVES?

1 Corinthians 9:19–23

My brothers didn't think I could survive an hour of aerobics. I knew *they* couldn't. So a friendly wager was on. We were on a cruise ship with some midnight buffets in the belly to burn off. So I ventured onto the gym floor and tried to mimic the moves of the instructor. Since I have the rhythm of an irregular heartbeat, I found it most challenging. But because my brothers were behind me, I kept kicking. An hour later, my brothers looked like they were going to a banquet. "Didn't you think the aerobics were hard?" I asked.

"Actually," my brother confessed, "we started, but we figured that if we looked half as dumb as you did, we wanted nothing to do with it. So we dropped out."

The only reason I persisted in my perspiring was because I assumed my brothers were behind me. Come to find out, I was exercising alone.

Do you suppose this is a parable of the church? We work hard and sweat through a tornado of the religious activities. We're frantically busy with our schools and clinics and summer camps and prayer meetings—but are we just talking to ourselves?

Shortly before moving to pastor the Walla Walla College Church, I was working on a master of business administration degree at a local university. One evening a classmate cornered me and said, "I hear you're moving to Walla Walla."

"Yes!" I said. "You've heard of it?"

"I used to live there—actually in a suburb of Walla Walla."

"Really? I didn't know Walla Walla was big enough to have its own suburb."

"We lived in College Place in a cul-de-sac with all Adventists."

"Adventists?" I asked, fearful of what was coming.

"Yeah, I think it's a religion or something. The only thing I know about them is that they don't do garage sales on Saturday. Isn't that weird?"

I smiled and nodded.

Then she asked, "So why are you moving there?"

"It's a job transfer," I said, hoping to cut the conversation.

"What kind of job do you do?"

"Well," I said, "I'm an Adventist pastor."

"Really? You're a pastor? You seem so . . . normal!"

That conversation still taunts me. How is it that a woman could live for years in a neighborhood comprised exclusively of Seventh-day Adventists and the only thing she knows about us is that we don't do garage sales on Saturday? It makes me wonder: Are we just talking to ourselves?

The apostle Paul wrestled with this question. Listen to his heart for people who were far from God:

> Though I am free and belong to no one, I have made myself a slave to everyone, to win as many as possible. To the Jews I became like a Jew, to win the Jews. To those under the law I became like one under the law (though I myself am not under the law), so as to win those under the law. To those not having the law I became like one not having the law (though I am not free from God's law but am under Christ's law), so as to win those not having the law. To the weak I became weak, to win the weak. I have become all things to all people so that by all possible means I might save some. I do all this for the sake of the gospel, that I may share in its blessings (1 Corinthians 9:19–24).

Early in my ministry, this passage kept me awake at night. It occurred to me that I didn't have any real friends outside of the church. I ate with Adventists. I worshiped with Adventists. I played with Adventists. I worked with Adventists. All of my friends were Adventists.

So I began to pray, "God, if You want me to witness to lost people, where would I even begin?" That's when I had an epiphany. *Oh, I know where lost people hang out! The bowling alley!*

So I joined The Lousy Bowlers League—that seemed about my speed. Of course, no one on our team was as lousy as me. It didn't matter since I was only there to build relationships with people far from God.

Now, I don't mean for this to be judgmental, but it seemed as though everyone on our team was "lost." They cussed like lost people (mostly at me). They drank like lost people. They smoked like lost people. They told dirty jokes like lost people. I can't lie—the jokes were funny. Really funny. Inappropriate to repeat, but gut-hurting hilarious. I'd laugh. Then I'd feel guilty. Then I'd confess my sin but crack up all over again when the jokes came to mind. It got messy.

I would get home past midnight, reeking of smoke, reeling from the lunacy of it all. I would pray, "God, what is the point? Nobody is interested. Besides, You and I both know that bowling is not my spiritual gift."

In that den of doubt, it felt as though God was saying, "Karl, when you are in that bowling alley with a heart to befriend people that do not know Me, it is in that place where you are most squarely in the sweet spot of My will."

I wish the end of my story mirrored that of a typical Adventist evangelist. You know how the story is supposed to end: "So I baptized everyone on the team. Then I baptized all the other teams in the league. Then I baptized all the other leagues and we transformed the bowling alley into a megachurch. Oh, and the last person I baptized was the manager of the bowling alley whom you know today as Ted Wilson, president of the General Conference of Seventh-day Adventists."

That's how it's *supposed* to end. The truth is, my bowling evangelism rendered one pseudospiritual conversation. A buddy told me he was going through a divorce. I suggested that he attend a meeting in my church called Lost Relationships Support Group. I offered to take him. He agreed, but a couple hours before I was to pick him up he called and flaked, saying something about not being "a church guy."

So that's the closest I would ever come to influencing my team for Jesus. Pitiful, huh?

I understand why many churches settle in after a while with the unpublished mission statement that says, "We just want to talk to ourselves."

It is so much easier to play church and let our spiritual busyness pass for doing the mission Jesus gave us.

Jesus felt so passionate about this mission that one time He shared the same story, back to back to back in rapid-fire succession, to hammer home one point: Lost people matter to God.

Do you remember the stories? A shepherd had one hundred sheep. One went AWOL, but that sheep mattered to the shepherd. So he left the ninety-nine in peril to search for the one. When he found that missing sheep, he invited his friends and neighbors to a party. Then they celebrated because the lost sheep was found!

A woman had ten coins. She lost one of them. But the coin mattered to her so she launched an all-out search. When she found that coin, she invited her friends and neighbors to a party. And they celebrated because the lost coin was found!

A man had two sons. The younger one demanded his inheritance early and then squandered it. I don't have to tell you that the kid mattered to the dad. So every day the father waited, hoping his boy would find his way back home. When the lost son finally returned, the father pulled out all the stops and threw a party unlike anything the town had ever seen. And they celebrated because the lost son was found!

Taking a page out of Jesus' lesson plans, let's wrap up this chapter with three similar stories that remind us of God's number one priority—lost people.

Story one

Rachel and I met in a public-speaking class while getting our MBA degrees. Our first assignment was to meet someone new.

I swiveled to my left. "Hi, I'm Karl."

"Rachel," she said. "I work at Boeing. I'm not married, but I have a cat." She handed me a business card that listed an alphabet after her name—CPA, CFSA, and so on.

So began a friendship that continues to this day.

One night after class, she said abruptly, "You're a pastor, right?"

"Yes."

"So do you believe in God?"

"Yes."

"Could you tell me about God?"

My pulse doubled. I knew that eternity was hanging in the balance. Then I shared a simple gospel presentation and finished by saying, "We'd love to have you come visit our church some week."

"I'll think about it," she said.

Several months later, I glanced down from the pulpit to see Rachel and her boyfriend, Rick. After the service, I raced to the lobby to greet them.

"It's so good to see you!" I said.

"Well, we came Sunday morning," she said, "but nobody was here. You didn't tell me you meet on Saturdays." (I've never been big on details!)

"Sorry," I said, "but I'm so glad you found us."

Then she flashed some bling on her finger and said, "Guess what? Rick and I are getting married! I'm so disappointed because you're the only clergy guy I know, so I wanted you to do the service. But the ceremony is on Saturday. So far as I can tell, that's the only day you work."

"I wouldn't miss it," I said. "I'll be there. But hey, come back to church next week."

"Yeah, maybe we will. It wasn't as weird as I thought it would be."

The next Friday I noticed the church lawn had not been mowed. I called the deacon who told me the riding mower was broken and he would try to get at it the following week. Normally, that wouldn't have bothered me, but all I could think about was Rachel and Rick. What message would that send if the grounds were a wreck? You see, it's one thing to send out a mass mailing to faceless names and invite them to a prophecy seminar at church. It is different when we're trying to introduce our friends and family members to Jesus. We do church differently. Suddenly, it becomes personal.

I said to the deacon, "I have a couple friends that may visit our church tomorrow so we have to mow the lawn."

"But, Pastor, it's five acres."

"I don't care," I said. "Get some scissors. I'll help you."

So we mowed the lawn. Rick and Rachel showed up the next day.

For the next two years, they faithfully participated in our church. Then they attended a series of meetings hosted by Lonnie Melashenko, long-time speaker and director for *Voice of Prophecy*, the religious radio broadcast. One evening, I asked Rachel if she wanted to meet Lonnie. "Absolutely!" she said.

As we approached Elder Melashenko, Rachel raced ahead and said,

"Your hair is always so perfect. I just want to mess it up." With that, she lunged forward and swirled his impeccably coifed hair until he looked like Einstein. Lonnie stood in shock. Standing behind Rachel, I tried to gesture that I was trying to lead her to Christ.

Evangelism can get messy. Lonnie was a great sport, and we still laugh about it. During those meetings, we visited Rachel and Rick and asked them, "Have you ever thought about being baptized?"

They replied in perfect stereo, "We thought you'd never ask! We want to be baptized this Sabbath."

Standing in the baptistry with Rick and Rachel remains one of the most cherished memories of my ministry. In that moment, all of heaven erupted in a party because two of God's kids came home.

Story two

Fernando and Gail were derelicts of sorts. Fernando didn't have a job. Gail worked in the back of a sweatshop sewing motorcycle jackets.

As they tell their story, one day Fernando happened into the back of that shop. Not being one to waste words, Fernando said, "I find myself irresistibly attracted to you. What do you say we live together?"

Gail agreed, and things were going along fine until early one morning Gail said, "I think we should start going to church."

"Church?" Fernando asked.

"Yes."

"But we aren't church people!"

"I know," Gail said, "but I think that is what is missing in our lives."

They argued about it until finally they struck a bargain: Fernando would go to church with Gail if she would let him go back to sleep.

"Deal!" Gail was thrilled.

Scanning the Yellow Pages, Gail noticed a church with a funny name, Seventh-day Adventist. That got her wondering if "Seventh-day" meant they worshiped on Saturday, the seventh day of the week. She called. Sure enough, there's a church that meets on Saturday, not Sunday. This meant they could get to church a day earlier. Fernando was game for whatever day.

The next Saturday, Fernando and Gail steered their Harleys into the parking lot of a small Seventh-day Adventist church. "Welcome!" an elderly woman said. In her fifty-plus years of greeting folk at that church, she'd never seen anything like these bikers. She asked the obvious: "Are you visiting?"

"Yes," Gail said.

"Perfect! We have a class just for you. I think you'll like the teacher. His name is Brother Bill."

Ushering them into the sanctuary, Fernando and Gail slipped into the back pew as Brother Bill began. "Good morning. Welcome, glad you're here. Now, before we jump into the Sabbath School lesson, I wonder if anybody has a question?"

Fernando's hand shot up. "Yeah, I got a question. How come God kills little babies?"

"Um . . . well . . . yes! Great question," Brother Bill said. He then presented an impromptu Bible study on why there is evil in the world if God is supposed to be good.

When he finished sharing his answer, Brother Bill glanced at Fernando and asked, "Does that help?"

"Yes, thank you," Fernando said.

They attended that little Bible study week after week until Gail suggested they stay for church. "Sure," Fernando said. "I like them folk."

As fate would have it, they chose to stay the one week out of the year that the pastor preached on stewardship. That was the annual sermon where he let the saints have it! "The reason so many of you don't know God's blessings in your life is because you don't tithe. How can you expect God to bless if you are stealing from Him?" By the end of the sermon, the pastor's shirt was soaked in sweat.

Later that week, Gail said to Fernando, "I think we ought to pay tithe."

"On what?" Fernando said. "In order to pay tithe you need an income."

"I know," Gail said. "I make a little money at the sweatshop."

While Fernando wasn't keen on the idea, he couldn't control Gail. He could, however, make a scene and let God know He'd better keep His end of the bargain. So the following Sabbath, when the offering plate came by, Fernando stood up and held the tithe envelope heavenward. Shaking it with jerky jabs, he yelled, "OK God, now do Your stuff." All this drama in the divine hour!

Next week, no blessings. "See," Fernando said, "I told you it doesn't work."

Gail said, "We have to be patient."

The next week in church, Fernando repeated his demands. Shouting over the grandma butchering an offertory on the piano, Fernando stood and told God to do His stuff. Then he plunked the envelope into the plate and waited for God to RSVP.

But that next week, no blessings. This happened week after week, until Fernando was done. "It doesn't work," he said.

Gail said, "Maybe you ought to pay tithe on your little business."

"Fine," Fernando bargained. "This week we will tithe on anything I make as well. But if we don't get blessed the next week, we never tithe again. Deal?"

"Deal."

The next Sabbath they returned a portion of two incomes and, wouldn't you know it, the following week Fernando's little business doubled. And the next week his business doubled again. And again. And again.

For thirteen weeks in a row his business grew exponentially, doubling week after week, until Fernando became one of the most lucrative marijuana dealers in all of Southern California!

They set up an appointment to talk to the pastor. "We decided to start doing that tithe thing you preached about," they said, "and God has been blessing our socks off. Week after week, Fernando's business has been doubling—almost to the exact penny."

"Praise the Lord," the pastor said. "What kind of business is it?"

"Well . . . it's in agriculture."

"Really?"

"Yes," Gail said. "Fernando sells pot."

"Oh, um, well . . . OK." The pastor tried to stay composed.

"Hey, we know this is not right," they continued. "We're wondering if you'd marry us. And baptize us. And help us move away from here so we can start all over again and really live like Seventh-day Adventist Christians."

The pastor, of course, was thrilled to help. He baptized them, married them, and helped pack up their few possessions and relocate to another state.

Last I heard, Fernando and Gail were youth leaders in their local Adventist church. And all of heaven erupted in a party because two of God's kids came home.

Story three

"Excuse me, Pastor." The young woman tugged on my arm in the crowded church lobby. "I want to be baptized."

"Praise the Lord," I said. While her face looked familiar, I didn't even attempt a name. "That's wonderful. Um, I'm sorry, I should know you, but—"

"Oh, I'm Candie. I've been coming to your church, and I would like to become a Seventh-day Adventist."

"Great! Let's meet to make the arrangements."

Later that week, I reviewed the basic doctrines of our church with her. I mentioned spiritual gifts. "For example," I said, "one of my gifts is teaching, so I don't mind talking in front of people."

"I think that's my gift too."

"Really? Well then, um, would you be willing to share your story just before I baptize you on Sabbath?"

"I'd love to."

I never thought to ask her about her story.

The next Sabbath morning, Candie stood in the baptistry and began her story. "I was a teenage prostitute and worked for twelve years as a stripper."

I had never seen the members so attentive—certainly not during any of my sermons. My pulse doubled as I wondered where her story was going next.

"My dad disappeared before I can remember him. My mom was an alcoholic. My brother is in jail."

Candie spared the sordid details but shared enough for everyone to get that she had a lot of brokenness and pain. She quickly jumped to the topic of "God's mind-blowing, indescribable, amazing grace." Indeed, her spiritual gift was public speaking.

"If God's grace can cover me," she said, "then there is no such thing in God's vocabulary as an ineligible candidate. If God can change me, He can change anybody."

With that, I lowered Candie into the water. Everybody in the church stood and applauded for what seemed like fifteen minutes.

In that holy moment it hit me with fresh force—the power of God to forgive and transform a sinner. Only God can change a prostitute into a promise-keeper. Only Christ can reconstruct the composition of a human heart. Only He can stoop into the shadows and salvage the brokenness of a spiritual casualty like Candie, Fernando, Gail, Rick, Rachel, you, and me.

At the potluck lunch, I noticed that Candie was gone. "Have you seen Candie?" I asked several people. My wife looked in the restroom. I searched in nearby classrooms. No Candie.

Then I saw her. At the baptistry, she sat alone in a cavernous sanctuary.

"Are you OK?" I asked.

"Oh, hi Pastor," she said. "Yes, I've never been better."

"What are you doing?"

"Well, I just wanted to watch the water go down the drain. I can promise you this tank will never again hold this much sin. You know, Pastor, you may not be able to relate to this, but for the first time in my life, I feel clean. I have never felt this way before. Isn't God's grace amazing?"

And all of heaven erupted in a party because God's kid came home.

For reflection

1. Why do you suppose many of our churches drift toward an unpublished mission statement that says, "We just want to talk to ourselves"?
2. What do your neighbors know about your church? What would want them to know? What is the most winsome way you can share your faith with them?
3. What might it look like in your context to "become all things to all people so that by all possible means [you] might save some" (1 Corinthians 9:22)?
4. Which of the stories in Luke 15 resonates most with you? Why? If Jesus were telling three stories today that illustrate how much lost people matter to God, how might He adapt them to our context?
5. In the story of the prodigal son, with whom do you identify with the most—the father, the older brother, or the younger brother? Explain.
6. Read Matthew 22:1–10. Reflect: Do I inadvertently deem some people unworthy of God's kingdom? What does my answer suggest about me?
7. Ellen White says, "God has given us the gift of speech that we may recite to others His dealing with us, that His love and compassion may touch other hearts, and that praise may arise from other souls also to Him who has called them out of darkness into His marvelous light."[1] How is God calling you to use this "gift of speech" to share His grace?

---

1. Ellen G. White, *Counsels to Parents, Teachers, and Students* (Mountain View, CA: Pacific Press®, 1913), 243.

Chapter 2

ARE WE DRIFTING?

Matthew 28:19, 20; Acts 1:9–14

What do you suppose is the greatest danger facing our church? What might threaten our very existence—close our doors—shut us down for business?

I don't think it would be doctrinal in nature. Our denomination has published twenty-eight fundamental beliefs. They're carefully thought through. They're very biblical. I don't think doctrines will ultimately be our undoing.

I don't think it's organizational in nature. The Seventh-day Adventist Church is a very structured organization. I was reminded of this at the 2015 General Conference Session, a gathering of over seventy-five thousand Seventh-day Adventists from all around the world. We have conferences, unions, divisions, and the General Conference. Oh, we are organized all right.

You know what I think it is? I think it's missional in nature—what organizational gurus refer to as "mission drift," where we just get fuzzy on the focus; where we lose clarity on what we are called to be and what we are called to do; where we just get off track a bit from our original mission.

If we drift from our mission, our demise is certain. I don't think that's too strong, is it?

So what is our mission? Well, our Leader has articulated the "why" for our church in Matthew 28:18–20. We call it the Great Commission. That's where Jesus says, "Here's your mission." Just before He ascends to the Father, He says, "This is what I want you to be about." We are to go and reach lost people with the good news of Jesus Christ and then teach them the ways of Jesus. Reach and teach—baptize people in the name of the Father, the Son, and the Holy Spirit and then disciple them so that the character of Christ is fully formed in each person. That's our mission!

I like the title of a Sermon Spice video, "The Everyday Commission."[1] This is not a program; rather, it's a lifestyle. As one line in that video says, "You can live this mission as you are going." A lot of times we think the Great Commission is this grandiose, lofty ideal that's framed and hung on a wall somewhere. But it really doesn't seep in to the places we live and what we actually do.

So if there is a threat to the longevity of this church, I would say it's that we lose focus on the everyday mission that God has given us. So my question is, "Are we doing this?" Are we living the Great Commission each day? Or are we just providing great religious programming? Are we just talking to ourselves and enjoying community? Or are we really fulfilling "the everyday commission"?

It is not our mission to do lots and lots of good things, which we do. Our mission is to fulfill God's commission wherever we are—to reach lost people for the kingdom of God and then teach them the Jesus way of life. That is what we are about.

We need to ask ourselves the question about our church, "Does it beat with the heartbeat of its original Founder?" Here is that heartbeat: "Go, and make disciples in the name of the Father, the Son, and the Holy Spirit." This is our everyday commission.

Peter Greer and Chris Horst, in their book *Mission Drift: The Unspoken Crisis Facing Leaders, Charities, and Churches*, document how common it is for organizations to lose that original heartbeat of the founder. They write,

> Mission Drift unfolds slowly. Like a current, it carries organizations away from their core purpose and identity. . . .
>
> The pressures of Mission Drift are guaranteed. It is the default, the auto-fill. It *will happen* unless we are focused and actively preventing it.[2]

Mission drift will happen in every church unless we are actively preventing it. How do we prevent it from happening to us? What are we to do? I point us back to the story of Jesus giving this commission. Look at what the disciples do with Jesus' instructions.

"After he said this, he was taken up before their very eyes, and a cloud hid him from their sight. They were looking intently up into the sky as he was going, when suddenly two men dressed in white stood beside them. 'Men of Galilee,' they said, 'why do you stand here looking into the sky? This same Jesus, who has been taken from you into heaven, will come back in the same way you have seen him go into heaven' " (Acts 1:9–11).

You've probably heard the saying that Christians can be so heavenly minded they are of no earthly good. I think that comes from this conversation the two angels had with the disciples. "What are you doing? He just gave you your mission. Get to work. Don't stand here looking up into heaven. Get on mission!" So they do.

Now notice, the first thing they do is to get together. "Then the apostles returned to Jerusalem from the hill called the Mount of Olives, a Sabbath day's walk from the city. When they arrived, they went upstairs to the room where they were staying. . . . They all joined together constantly in prayer" (verses 12–14).

The first—and most important—factor in fulfilling "the everyday commission": "They devoted themselves to prayer." The next verse tells us there were about 120 of them there—praying together. So let's start there.

Recently, I was in a meeting when someone referenced a story in Max Lucado's book *Before Amen.* She shared how the story had transformed her little Baptist church. When our meeting ended, I bought the book.

Here's the story: Many years ago, Max Lucado received an invitation to speak at John Maxwell's church in San Diego. Lucado agreed to preach in exchange for Maxwell's best advice for building a healthy church. Lucado writes: "[John] was quick to give [his advice]: prayer. He specifically suggested that I recruit 120 prayer partners who would commit to pray daily for the church, me, and my family." Max went back to his church with the plan to recruit 120 prayer partners. Six months later, Max reported to John what had happened:

- "We had broken our Sunday attendance record twice.

- We had finished the year with our highest-ever average [church] attendance.
- We had finished the year well over budget.
- We had nearly doubled our staff and elders.
- We had witnessed several significant healings.
- Church antagonism was at an all-time low; and
- Church unity was at an all-time high."

Max goes on to state he was stunned! He said the church felt God's wind in their sails, and all they did was increase their resolve to pray.

Lucado concludes that story by saying this: "As we redouble our commitment to pray, God redoubles his promise to bless."[3]

So here's my challenge: Join an army of prayer warriors. Commit to God and one another that you will pray daily for your church, your leaders, and your families. Pray that God will protect your church from mission drift. Pray that you will remain mission true—focused solely on the mission to reach lost people and teach them how to live the Jesus way of life.

For reflection

1. What do you think is the greatest danger facing the church?
2. "If we, as a church, drift off mission, our demise is certain." Do you agree or disagree? Explain.
3. What is the mission of your life? Do you find yourself drifting off your mission? If so, in what way(s)?
4. How can you fulfill "the everyday commission" today?
5. How central is prayer in your church? In your life? How might you elevate the prominence of prayer?
6. What is there in your life that would make someone want to know more about Jesus?
7. Reflect on this statement: "Thousands can be reached in the most simple, humble way. The most intellectual, those who are looked upon as the world's most gifted men and women, are often refreshed by the simple words of one who loves God. . . . The true, honest expression of a son or daughter of God, spoken in natural simplicity, has power to open the door to hearts that have long been closed against Christ and His love."[4] Look for opportunities today to share Christ and His love with others.

---

1. "The Everyday Commission," No Limits Publishing, http://www.sermonspice.com/product/64397/the-everyday-commission.
2. Peter Greer and Chris Horst, *Mission Drift: The Unspoken Crisis Facing Leaders, Charities, and Churches* (Bloomington, MN: Bethany House, 2014), 18, 30, 31 (italics in the original).
3. Max Lucado, *Before Amen: The Power of a Simple Prayer* (Nashville, TN: Thomas Nelson, 2014), 75–77.
4. Ellen G. White, *The Colporteur Evangelist* (Mountain View, CA: Pacific Press®, 1920), 38.

Chapter 3

WHY DON'T THOSE MIRACLES HAPPEN IN MY CHURCH?

Acts 16:6–34

In his classic book *Fresh Wind, Fresh Fire*, Pastor Jim Cymbala tells of arriving at the Brooklyn Tabernacle to try and revive the church. The building was in disrepair. Attendance had dwindled. Finances had dried up. The dying church had a Do Not Resuscitate order. Then Super Pastor swoops into town. Miracles become as common as fruit flies. And now they are happy all the day

To be fair, it is an inspiring story of God's supernatural power. But books such as that always make me wonder, *Why don't we experience the same miracles, growth, and blow-your-mind stories in my church?*

That same question hits me when I read about the early Christian church. Acts 16:5 reports how "the churches were strengthened in the faith and grew daily in numbers." Is that how you would describe your church? Daily growing in faith and numbers? If so, your church is the outlier. Sadly, most churches are declining daily.

There was a time, however, when the church was ground zero for God's miracles. Acts 16 records three such stories. Notice the preface for these miracles.

"Paul and his companions traveled throughout the region of Phrygia and Galatia, having been kept by the Holy Spirit from preaching the word in the province of Asia. When they came to the border of Mysia, they tried to enter Bithynia, but the Spirit of Jesus would not allow them to. So they passed by Mysia and went down to Troas" (verses 6–8).

Here Paul is heading to Bithynia and God scrambles the GPS directions and sends him to Troas instead. I think of this scene whenever I'm heading somewhere to preach. I imagine leaving this voice mail: "Hey Elder Smith, I know you're expecting me in Arizona tonight for camp meeting, but I just got a prompting from the Holy Spirit to go to Bophuthatswana instead. OK, hope it goes well."

Because Paul and his buddies were so dialed in to God's directions, they changed their itinerary. What follows are three miracle stories.

Miracle one: Lydia

Luke writes, "On the Sabbath we went outside the city gate to the river, where we expected to find a place of prayer. We sat down and began to speak to the women who had gathered there. One of those listening was a woman from the city of Thyatira named Lydia, a dealer in purple cloth. She was a worshiper of God. The Lord opened her heart to respond to Paul's message. When she and the members of her household were baptized, she invited us to her home. 'If you consider me a believer in the Lord,' she said, 'come and stay at my house.' And she persuaded us" (verses 13–15).

Lydia sat atop the social ladder. As a dealer in purple products, she was a wealthy woman who wielded great influence. Consider this: the purple dye had to be painstakingly gathered drop by drop from a rare shellfish. To dye a pound of wool would cost about $350 in today's currency. So this would be like baptizing your local Porsche dealer and her entire family. That would qualify as a miracle, don't you think?

So I ask again, "Why doesn't this happen every day in my church?"

Miracle two: The demon-possessed slave

The miracles keep coming. Look at the next story. "Once when we were going to the place of prayer, we were met by a female slave who had a spirit by which she predicted the future. She earned a great deal of money for her owners by fortune-telling. She followed Paul and the rest of us, shouting, 'These men are servants of the Most High God, who are telling you the way to be saved' " (verses 16, 17).

Here we meet a woman on the opposite extreme from Lydia. In the ancient world, she had three major strikes against her. She was a woman.

She was a slave. She was demon possessed. From her social standing, this woman was looking up at dogs, pigs, and, of course, all people. And yet, God still used her as an evangelist! She testifies that Paul and his friends "are servants of the Most High God." If God can use this woman to fulfill "the everyday commission," surely He can use you and me.

Her relentless preaching so annoyed Paul that "he turned around and said to the spirit, 'In the name of Jesus Christ I command you to come out of her!' At that moment the spirit left her" (verse 18).

Many years ago, a woman stormed into my office and introduced herself as a "servant of Satan." Teaming up with a couple elders, we held an exorcism. Quoting Paul, I said, "In the name of Jesus Christ I command you to come out of her!"

Nothing happened.

We repeated the command for good measure, but her torment only heightened. Which leaves me to wonder: *Why did God cast out demons in the ancient church, but in my church today He seems disinterested or powerless?*

Miracle three: The jailer

The next miracle is even more impressive. The crowds threw Paul and Silas into "the inner cell" and their feet were "fastened in the stocks."

> About midnight Paul and Silas were praying and singing hymns to God, and the other prisoners were listening to them. Suddenly there was such a violent earthquake that the foundations of the prison were shaken. At once all the prison doors flew open, and everyone's chains came loose. The jailer woke up, and when he saw the prison doors open, he drew his sword and was about to kill himself because he thought the prisoners had escaped. But Paul shouted, "Don't harm yourself! We are all here!"
>
> The jailer called for lights, rushed in and fell trembling before Paul and Silas. He then brought them out and asked, "Sirs, what must I do to be saved?"
>
> They replied, "Believe in the Lord Jesus, and you will be saved—you and your household." Then they spoke the word of the Lord to him and to all the others in his house. At that hour of the night the jailer took them and washed their wounds; then immediately he

> and all his household were baptized. The jailer brought them into his house and set a meal before them; he was filled with joy because he had come to believe in God—he and his whole household (verses 24–34).

If Lydia was at the top of the social scale and the slave girl at the bottom, this man was part of the Roman civil service—which is to say, he was squarely in the middle class. In Acts 16, we find the full socio-economic spectrum. In other words, God's miracles are open to all—rich, poor, black, white, Christian, non-Christian, Republicans, Democrats, and everything in between.

The Almighty does not discriminate. He longs to perform the same miracles for you and for your faith community. So why, then, do we not share similar stories every day in church?

Here's a better question: What can we learn from Paul and Silas to build a similar culture that would be conducive to God performing the same kinds of miracles? Are there common denominators in these three miracle stories that would create a similar environment for God to work today? While we cannot manipulate the Almighty, we can do the same things today that the believers did in the early church. Who knows? God may bless us in the same way.

So how do we cultivate a culture that is conducive to the church being strengthened in faith and growing daily in numbers? Note three habits (that we can practice today!) that are central to the stories.

Habit one: Look in

First, we can cultivate a conversation with the Holy Spirit. Simply put, look in. Be receptive and responsive to the promptings of God's Spirit.

The Holy Spirit played *the* central role in this revival. Remember how the travel schedule was changed by the Holy Spirit? Because Paul and his teammates were so tuned in to the Holy Spirit, they experienced miracles beyond their loftiest expectations.

If we are to experience another revival, then we must cultivate an ongoing conversation with the Holy Spirit. Ellen White writes: "A revival of true godliness among us is the greatest and most urgent of all our needs. We must have the holy unction from God, the baptism of his Spirit. . . . It is the Spirit of God that quickens the lifeless faculties of the soul to appreciate heavenly things, and attracts the affections toward God and the truth."[1]

Unless we nurture this conversation with the Spirit and do God's biddings, we cannot experience revival. This truth hit home on a recent trip when I was working on this chapter. As I settled into my seat on the plane, I wondered, *God, what would it look like for me to foster this ongoing conversation with You? What surprises and miracles might be in store for me?*

Just then, a woman hurried up from the back of the plane and settled into her new seat next to me. I sensed God telling me to speak to her. It wasn't an audible voice, but it was as clear a prompting as I've ever felt.

But God, I thought, *You know I hate talking to strangers on the plane. This is why I always wear the universal symbol that screams "DO NOT TALK TO ME!"—noise-canceling headphones.*

The prompting was intense and unrelenting. *"Karl, you asked Me what it would look like to live in constant dialogue with Me. So if you want the same kind of miracles that you read about in the early Christian church, then I'm telling you what you need to do. Talk to this woman."*

But what would I say?

"Maybe start by introducing yourself."

No, that feels weird.

Back and forth the inner dialogue went when the woman asked a very random question. Skipping the usual pleasantries, she started with the question, "Are you a priest?"

I shook my head. The one problem with noise-canceling headphones is that you can still hear what people say to you.

"Are you a rabbi?" she asked.

Again, I shook my head.

"Are you a pastor?"

Sliding the headphones down, I resigned myself to the inevitable. "Yes. I am a pastor," I said. "Have we met before?"

"No," she said. "I just knew that when they gave me a new seat assignment it was God's way of reminding me that He has not forsaken me. So I figured my new seatmate would work for God."

Stunned, I asked about her story.

"Well," she sighed, "I am returning from three days of saying goodbye to my brother. He has leukemia. The doctors say there is nothing more they can do. I hardly slept or ate anything for the past three days.

I am spiritually, emotionally, physically, and mentally exhausted. So I just knew God was going to remind me that I'm not going through this alone."

For the next two hours, we talked. We shared about our families, careers, churches, cancer, politics, world events, and why bad things happen to good people. When our plane landed, she thanked me for listening and praying for her brother. She gave me a hearty hug and promised to keep me updated on her brother's battle.

Later she sent me this text: "Karl, being able to share with you on that flight meant so much to me. God used you to bring such comfort. Michael lost his fight with leukemia. He was a wonderful man/brother/father who loved the Lord and is very much missed. Thanks so much for being there when I desperately needed to know that God had not forsaken me. Ours was a divine appointment. May you continue to shine the light of Jesus in this dark world."

I wonder how many of these miracles I've missed because I won't take off my noise-canceling headphones. How many times do I drown out that still, small voice? Understand this: revival happens when God's people listen to the Spirit and then act.

Habit two: Look up

The second critical piece of the early church revival is prayer. This means cultivating a conversation with God. Simply put, look up. Let's review the centrality of prayer in the three stories.

In the story of Lydia, it says, "On the Sabbath we went outside the city gate to the river, where we expected to find a place of prayer" (verse 13). Then in the next story, we read, "Once when we were going to the place of prayer, we were met by a female slave who had a spirit" (verse 16). In the jailer's case, we see that at "about midnight Paul and Silas were praying and singing hymns to God" (verse 25). Prayer is a key factor in the success of the early church.

Still today, prayer is central to any revival. Jim Cymbala said to his congregation at the Brooklyn Tabernacle, "The prayer meeting will be the barometer of our church. What happens on Tuesday night will be the gauge by which we will judge success or failure because that will be the measure by which God blesses us."

Pastor Cymbala goes on to tell of a visiting pastor who came to his church and shared this observation: "You can tell how popular a church is by who comes on Sunday morning. You can tell how popular the pastor or evangelist is by who comes on Sunday night. But you can tell how popular Jesus is by who comes to the prayer meeting."[2]

Habit three: Look out

Another common theme in the stories is the focus beyond self. Lydia influenced "the members of her household" (verse 15) to follow Jesus. Even the slave girl testified to others that Paul was sharing the way of salvation (verse 17). In the jailer's story, he, too, influenced "all his household" (verse 33) to be baptized.

What would happen if we were to live with the same outward focus? What if we peered beyond our self-centered worlds and seized opportunities to serve and give and help others? Maybe we could spark a kingdom revolution!

Another airplane experience comes to mind. Having traveled a fair bit, I am fluent in "Airlinese." So the other day at O'Hare International Airport when the agent announced, "Hey folks, it looks like flight 4474 is delayed. Maintenance is on their way to fix a flat tire. This should just take a few minutes so please stay near our gate," I could correctly translate this. "Hey folks, if you'd like to get up and move around Chicago, this would be a good time to do so. I heard *Hamilton* is playing downtown at the CIBC Theatre."

Three hours later, they let on board military, global service, first class, and anyone needing extra assistance. To be fair, on this flight, the airline (which shall remain anonymous) did upgrade me—causing mild guilt for my many online rants through the years I tagged #Don'tFlyUnited.

I settled into my ever-so-cushy seat while the attendant poured me a glass (and I do mean glass) of water. That's when I overheard the pilot say, "No, this is a different issue. Sorry, but we can't have passengers on board while they fix it." Airlinese translation: "Go wait three more hours."

I sat statuesque—half in shock, half in anger—tempted to make their security guards come and violently drag me off the plane. At the very least, I determined to be the last passenger sitting.

Suddenly, a blonde girl (who I guessed to be about ten) burst on the scene. She performed a perfect reverse belly flop into the seat in front of me. Throwing her hands high in the air like a ref signaling a touchdown, she shouted, "So this is what first class feels like! Grandma, look at me!"

Grandma inched toward a wheelchair waiting for her on the jet bridge. "Oh my!" she said. "Wendalyn, you can't be in that seat."

"There's enough room for both of us. Come sit with me, Grandma. This is like flying Beanbag Airlines!"

"Come along, Wendalyn. They need us to get off the plane so they can make it safe."

"One day, I'm going to fly first class."

"Well," Grandma said, "these seats are only for really rich people."

"OK then, I guess I need to get really rich because some day I'm gonna sit up here with the bagillionaires."

True to my vow, I was the last passenger to get off. And just as I figured, their "few minutes" stretched into three more hours of stewing at the gate. I should have visited *Hamilton*. Instead, I went to the agent at the desk to broker a deal with the seating map.

When we finally boarded again, I sat in coach and watched with pure joy as the attendant explained to Wendalyn how her seat was changed from 16A to 2B. At first, confusion contorted her face, giving way in short order to a 1,000-watt smile. She shuffled forward as if trying to prolong this dream.

From my seat, I could see through the blue mesh curtain into the cabin of bagillionaires. I couldn't contain my giddy glee in watching the attendant serve Wendalyn a dozen glasses of Coke. Then she insisted on a selfie with every one of her new rich friends.

When we landed, she called her mom. She didn't seem to care if everyone on the plane could hear her. "Mom, you will never guess where I am . . . No! I'm not still at the airport. I'm in first class! . . . That's right, I said first class, with a bunch of really rich people. They're all nice though . . . Of course I ate the meal, and one of my new rich friends didn't want her cookie so I had two cookies . . . And the guy told me that in first class you get all the Coke you can drink . . . No, Grandma had to sit back there with all the poor people . . . Yes, I'll wait for her, but I want to be the last one to get off . . . I love you too."

Like I said, I've traveled a fair bit. But this was my favorite flight of all time. In fact, I'm still flying high.

Making miracles happen

Maybe the miracle stories aren't so out of reach after all. Perhaps God wants our church today to flourish in the same way as it did in the first century.

It can happen if all of us sign on for "the everyday commission." This is not some lofty ideal that can never be accomplished in real life. Rather, it is God's grandest desire to grow His church in faith and numbers.

So what's it going to take?

Ordinary folk like you and me who commit to three simple, daily disciplines:

- **Look in**—Pay attention to the promptings of the Spirit. When He urges you to do something, do it!
- **Look up**—"Pray continually," the apostle Paul urges (1 Thessalonians 5:17). As you manage your ordinary day, keep a continuous conversation with Jesus going.
- **Look out**—God calls you to live beyond yourself. Take every opportunity to serve others.

Do these things today, and God may just show up and surprise you with miracles aplenty!

For reflection

1. Read the book of Acts. How is the church today similar to the early Christian church? How is it different?
2. What one thing about the early Christian church you would like to see God replicate in your church today?
3. Have you ever experienced a miracle? Share your stories in a small group.
4. Compare the three miracles highlighted in this chapter (Lydia, the demon-possessed slave, the jailer). What similarities are there in the stories? What are some of the differences?
5. Make today an experiment. Listen for promptings from the Holy Spirit and then act on these biddings. How does being mindful of God's Spirit guiding you in the moment impact the way you live?
6. When Paul commands us to "pray without ceasing" (1 Thessalonians 5:17, KJV), what does that mean? What does it *not* mean?
7. Write down ten ways you can serve others this week. Try to complete your list. Invite a friend to join you in this adventure of service and then at the end of the week, share your stories of what happened.

---

1. Ellen G. White, *Gospel Workers* (Battle Creek, MI: Review and Herald®, 1892), 370.
2. Jim Cymbala, "Catching Fire," *World Challenge Blogspot*, November 9, 2013, http://davidwilkersontoday.blogspot.com/2013/11/catching-fire-by-jim-cymbala.html.

Chapter 4

HOW CAN I WITNESS WITHOUT BEING A WEIRDO?

John 4:1–19, 39

Christians [often] come off as pushy or plain weird," writes Yurik Strasyuk. Sad, but true, isn't it? He continues:

> **We often expect evangelism to be a loud, exciting, grandiose movement that makes the Christian newspaper, instead of a quiet, normal friendship that gets no applause.** We want to rely on certain evangelistic systems, but minimize our reliance on Jesus. Yet instead of focusing on thousands of converts, why not focus on being a good friend to one person? *We see so many churches that are shrinking. If every Christian simply loved one friend to Jesus, once in their life, Churches would continually double!*[1]

"Sharing your faith" is not about winning an argument. It's about loving our friends to Jesus. So how can we do this in a winsome way? Well, let's look at the Master Himself.

The first six verses in John 4 set up the context for a story that highlights the "how" of being a winning witness. John writes, "Now Jesus learned that the Pharisees had heard that he was gaining and baptizing more disciples than John—although in fact it was not Jesus who baptized, but his disciples" (John 4:1, 2). The church leaders were bothered because Jesus was modeling His mission. What was this mission? To baptize people (although the text explains that He let His disciples do the actual baptizing) and teach them the kingdom way of life.

"So he left Judea and went back once more to Galilee. Now he had to go through Samaria" (verses 3, 4). Don't skim over the detail that Jesus *"had"* to go through Samaria. If you were a rabbi in Judea and set your GPS unit to take you to Galilee, it would not take you through Samaria. For Jews in the ancient world, GPS stood for "Geographically Protected from Samaria." Their GPS units were set to avoid Samaria.

Similar, I suppose, to the trip we took last Christmas when our family splurged on a vacation to Europe. We rented a car and drove from Prague to Salzburg. What should have been a four-hour drive stretched into eight hours. We drove some dirt roads that made us wish we had rented a four-wheel drive. It wasn't until our return to Prague that we noticed the GPS unit was set to avoid toll roads (even though we had prepaid all tolls). So on the return, we cut the travel time in half!

Well, for Jews, such as Jesus and His disciples, they were programmed to go around Samaria—even though it meant twice the travel time. Nevertheless, Jesus *had* to go through Samaria.

"So he came to a town in Samaria called Sychar, near the plot of ground Jacob had given to his son Joseph. Jacob's well was there, and Jesus, tired as he was from the journey, sat down by the well. It was about noon" (verses 5, 6). The scene is now set for us to learn from the Master Evangelist on how to witness without the weirdness. Consider four tips.

1. Start with a question. "When a Samaritan woman came to draw water, Jesus said to her, 'Will you give me a drink?' " (verse 7).

If you want to share your faith, take a page from Jesus' evangelism notebook and start with a question. This is a disarming way to connect with people. Randy Newman, in his book *Questioning Evangelism*, makes a convincing case for putting questions at the center of our witnessing efforts. He writes,

> We can have better results from our evangelizing. Our efforts can produce more fruit, advancing the kingdom further than has been recently achieved. A better way exists, and it looks, sounds, and feels more like Jesus, the rabbi, than like . . . [a] used-car salesman. It involves more listening than speaking, inviting rather than demanding a decision. Perhaps the most important component to

this kind of evangelism is answering questions with questions rather than giving answers.[2]

Jesus understood the power of questions. After all, when you ask a question, the response will inform you as to deeper spiritual interest. Had the woman answered, "Get your own drink," no doubt Jesus would have respected her boundaries. Throughout the New Testament, if someone slammed the door on Jesus, He wiped the dust off His feet and moved on. He didn't barge through the door, nor should we. So start with a question and let the answer inform the way you proceed.

Brian Fikkert, in his book *When Helping Hurts*, provides a picture of this. Fikkert tells of the time he enrolled in a witnessing class at his Presbyterian church. They were given the assignment to "evangelize" an under-resourced, mostly African-American neighborhood. Their approach was to start with questions to discern spiritual interest. Fikkert writes,

> Each member of the class individually went door-to-door, saying to people, "Hello, I am from Community Presbyterian Church, the church just around the corner. We are conducting a survey today to find out what gifts God has placed in this community. What skills and abilities do you have?"
>
> The truth is that I wanted to die. Racial tensions are still very present in our city, so I knew there would be at least some social discomfort for both the African-American residents of this housing project and for me. Furthermore, [at seven feet tall] my height can be quite startling and intimidating, adding awkwardness to virtually all first encounters. And finally, the words I was supposed to repeat sounded totally hokey to me. "Hello, I am from Community Presbyterian Church, the church just . . ." Yuck! I would rather be selling Girl Scout cookies. . . . But alas, I had chosen this class, so off I dutifully marched and knocked on the first door.[3]

A five-foot-two, thirty-something African-American woman cracked open the door. Fikkert started in on his canned speech. "Hello, I am from Community Presbyterian Church . . . What skills do you have? What are you good at doing?"

As you might imagine, the woman was incredulous. Repeatedly, she said, "What?"

Just then, a voice came out of the dark behind her. "She can cook chitlins like there is no tomorrow!" Another voice yelled, "Yeah, ain't nobody can cook as good as she can!" A smile slowly formed as she admitted, "Yes, I think I can cook."

Fikkert writes,

> Next thing I knew, I found myself sitting in the living room with about six African Americans gathered around. . . .
>
> "This is Joe, he can fix bikes. Whenever one of the kids in the project has a bike that needs fixing, Joe is the man." A smile spread across Joe's face. "And this here is Mac. How is your car running? If you ever have trouble with your car, bring it right here to Mac." I noticed that Mac started to sit up a little straighter in his chair. They went on and on, bragging about one another to me. All I had to do was sit there and write it all down.[4]

As you become more intentional about living on mission and sharing Jesus with people who don't know Him, start by asking questions.

Richard Phillips puts it this way:

> Many Christians today wall themselves off from the world the way the Jews of Jesus' time did. Just as the Jews chose to bypass Samaria to avoid defilement, we tend to travel only within our own subculture. If we interact with worldly people, we certainly don't think they have anything to offer us. Small wonder, then, that they are not open to what we have to offer them. Jesus was not like that: He walked through the world and treated even a scandalous Samaritan woman as a person of worth, capable of giving Him something of value. As Frederick Godet wisely notes, "He is not unaware that the way to gain a soul is often to ask a service of it."[5]

2. Shift the conversation to spiritual matters. The second thing that Jesus does so masterfully in this exchange is to shift the conversation from the material realm of literal water to the spiritual realm of living water. In verse 9, the woman says, " 'You are a Jew and I am a Samaritan woman. How can you ask me for a drink?' (For Jews do not associate with Samaritans.)"

But notice how Jesus reframes everything by replying, "If you knew the gift of God and who it is that asks you for a drink, you would have asked him and he would have given you living water" (verse 10).

Jesus senses her spiritual curiosity, so He speaks of "living water." Jesus is seeding her imagination by comparing the difference between well water and living water—the difference between the material world and the spiritual world.

Rather than assuming this five-time divorcee would have no interest in spiritual things, Jesus "tests the waters." He uses a metaphor that stirs her spiritual curiosity.

The take-home here is never to write off people as spiritually hopeless or disinterested. You never know what God is doing in another person's heart.

On a recent trans-Atlantic flight, I sat next to a professional basketball player. While I couldn't place him on a team or recall his name, I knew he played in the National Basketball Association. If ever I assumed a preacher bringing God into the conversation would offend somebody, it was on that flight with that very tall man. So, I said nothing to him.

I noticed that the movie he selected from a generous menu of options was *War Room* a story about prayer and spiritual warfare. Several hours later, when I scrolled through the movie list, he introduced himself and said, "If you're looking for a great movie, I recommend *War Room.*"

"Really?" I said, surprised by his enthusiasm for such an overtly Christian movie.

"I've seen it," I said. "I'm a pastor, and we actually showed it at my church."

"That's awesome!" he said.

Sensing an opportunity to turn our talk toward spiritual matters, I asked him about his spiritual upbringing.

"Well," he said, "my grandma raised me. She was a very devoted Christian. I mean she went to church every night and all day on Sunday. I have to confess that I've drifted far from the way she tried to raise me. Playing in the NBA, it's hard to get to church, especially during the season."

What followed was a confession of the ways in which he had royally messed up in life, his desperate desire to make Jesus the Lord of his life, and his need for the courage to do the right thing by his "illegitimate daughter." Just before our plane landed, he asked if I would pray for him. I assured him that I would.

"No," he said, "I don't mean 'someday' in your prayer closet. I need you to pray for me right now."

So as the other passengers were adjusting their seatbacks and trays, we were bowing our heads to connect this seeker with his Savior. While this was not the landing I had anticipated, it was a memorable display of God at work in the heart of an improbable prodigal coming home.

Here's the point: always be open to spiritual opportunities! This is "the everyday commission." You never have to force faith into conversations, but if you are receptive and responsive to God's promptings, you will have many chances to share Jesus.

3. Share the benefits of faith. Once the conversation takes a spiritual turn, be ready to talk about the benefits of faith. Again, we learn this technique from Jesus.

> "Sir," the woman said, "you have nothing to draw with and the well is deep. Where can you get this living water? Are you greater than our father Jacob, who gave us the well and drank from it himself, as did also his sons and his livestock?"
>
> Jesus answered, "Everyone who drinks this water will be thirsty again, but whoever drinks the water I give them will never thirst. Indeed, the water I give them will become in them a spring of water welling up to eternal life" (verses 11–14).

Jesus shamelessly extols the benefits of a life with Him. He promises to quench the deep spiritual thirst that ravages every human soul. Jesus offers a better way to navigate life. So when you're sharing your faith, talk about these benefits.

Whenever I tell people that I am a Seventh-day Adventist, it's not unusual for someone to reply, "You're the church that can't eat ham, right?" Or, "You don't drink coffee, do you?" Sadly, too often our lifestyle practices get framed in a negative way. But think about what a golden witnessing tool our health message could be. After all, we can offer people what they want more than anything.

As Seventh-day Adventists, we can share this good news: "You can significantly increase your odds of adding an extra seven to fourteen years to your life and be healthier and happier besides. Would you like to add more years to your life and more life to your years?" Who wouldn't be interested in such a deal?

This is not some pie-in-the-sky claim. In the book *CREATION Health Discovery*, Doctors Des Cummings and Monica Reed use the acronym CREATION to outline eight guidelines to obtain a better life. They write:

> The CREATION Health model is the . . . foundation of the Adventist Health System. These eight principles have been practiced by hundreds of thousands of people over the last century and have resulted in national studies concluding that following these principles can add 7–14 years to your life. These studies have also demonstrated that following the eight principles brings about a significant reduction in the risk of lifestyle diseases such as cancer, stroke, and heart disease. By following the CREATION Health principles, Adventists have become known as the healthiest people in the world.[6]

When sharing this with seekers and nonbelievers, I am always quick to point out that as Adventists we do not believe that a healthy lifestyle is an issue of salvation. We do not believe that we are saved by eating tofu and FriChik. No! We are saved by the sacrifice Jesus made on the cross. Period. But I am also quick to say Adventists live longer.

Similarly, Jesus spoke to the benefits of following Him—"Drink of this living water and you will never thirst again." So share your spiritual convictions in the same way Jesus did. Accentuate the positive. Stress the benefits.

4. Offer unconditional acceptance. The final suggestion on how to share your faith without being weird is to accept all people, no matter where they are in their spiritual journey. Nobody is disqualified from God's grace.

I love how Jesus so delicately goes to the dark spaces of this woman's life, and He does it in a way in which she is neither offended nor defensive. Oh, that we could reach lost people with similar grace and tact! Just watch and admire the Master Evangelist in action:

> The woman said to him, "Sir, give me this water so that I won't get thirsty and have to keep coming here to draw water."
>
> He told her, "Go, call your husband and come back."
>
> "I have no husband," she replied.
>
> Jesus said to her, "You are right when you say you have no husband. The fact is, you have had five husbands, and the man you now have is not your husband. What you have just said is quite true."
>
> "Sir," the woman said, "I can see that you are a prophet. Our ancestors worshiped on this mountain, but you Jews claim that the place where we must worship is in Jerusalem" (verses 15–19).

Jesus takes a potentially awkward moment and ever so graciously addresses a very sensitive mess in her life—and He does this without her feeling shamed or disgraced.

Here's the deal about this woman: she has a story. Everybody has a story.

I doubt she dreamed as a little girl that one day she'd waste five marriages. Keep in mind, in the ancient world a woman did not have the right to initiate divorce. We think of this woman as scandalous, but mostly she was a victim. She met a man who made a promise. Then came the rejection: "No, I don't want you after all."

Five times she endured such betrayal. The boyfriend she is with at the time of this conversation most likely won't marry her. Still, Jesus treats her with such tender dignity. Here is a man, at last, who does not reject her.

Every person you talk with about Jesus has a story. The chapter titles vary: "Shame," "Regret," "Dishonor," "Guilt," "Sin," and so on. But the narrative is the same. We have all screwed up. And we all need grace. We all need acceptance.

So Jesus planted His church. Now He calls us to model the love, acceptance, and forgiveness that He showed to *all* people. Everyone is welcome in the church of Jesus.

But even the early church struggled to accept all people. So Paul addressed this issue in his letter to the Romans. He tells the saints in no uncertain terms that the church must be a community that accepts all people. Listen to his message of welcome from the KHV (Karl Haffner Version):

> At our church, we accept one another. We especially welcome you if you are weak in faith, high on drugs, or down in the dumps. If you have questions about the Holy Spirit, Allah, Jesus, Buddha, or the Kardashians, you've come to the right place. We don't care if you're pre-trib, post-trib, or no-trib. If you're a disciple of Dr. Phil, Dr. Drew, Dr. Oz, Dr. McCoy, Dr. Doolittle, or Dr. Seuss, welcome! Glad you're here. If you think pro wrestling is real and Elvis is alive and twenty-something blondes are really in love with ninety-year-old billionaires, then you've come to the right church. Make yourself at home.
>
> Whether you're a vegetarian or a carnivore, we have a place for you at the table. Some folks around here eat snakes, pigs, turtles, monkeys, and spotted owls, but they won't lord their foodie freedoms over you—even if you're on a strict bean and barley diet. No matter your tastes, we love you.
>
> We accept Sunday keepers, Sabbatarians, Wednesday worshipers, and Moonies. We respect your right to believe as you wish, eat as you might, and worship how you will.
>
> Come as you are. Sport your tats, piercings, dreads, threads, and Keds. Bring your fears, fetishes, frets, anxieties, biases, manias, doubts, qualms, and quirks. Read your Bible or your smartphone or your abacus. We don't care—we're just glad you're here! (Romans 14:1–6; my paraphrase).

I suspect that if churches would throw down a welcome mat like that, people would be trampling over each other to get inside. You see, there are a couple of approaches that churches can take when it comes to evangelism. One method is to invite all people to come and share in the Living Water. The other approach sets up barriers to assure the purity of God's people.

The two approaches can be illustrated by the dilemma cattle ranchers face in Australia. Since the farms are massive, ranchers must decide, "How do we keep the cattle on the ranch?" Basically, there are two ways of doing this. They can build a fence around the property. Or, they can dig a well.

The fence option is often prohibitively expensive. But it does work. The other option, placing a well at the heart of the ranch, is so life-giving and refreshing and rejuvenating that cows want to stay at the watering hole.

A lot of churches are into building fences. This is not new. In Jesus' day, the rabbis would talk about building a fence around the Torah. The idea being, "Let's keep the good people who obey God's commandments safe from the riffraff like the Samaritans. We dare not be defiled by the heathens 'out there,' so we'll build fences to keep them out and keep our own safe 'in here.' "

But Jesus redefined spirituality. "What defiles people," He taught, "is not what touches them from the outside; it's what happens on the inside. Live in an intimate relationship with Me, drink of the Living Water, feast on the Bread of Life, and your soul will experience the refreshing, rejuvenating Spirit of life. And you won't want to wander anywhere else."

Here's my paraphrase of His promise:

> Drink the water of this world, and you'll find it as refreshing as swallowing sand.
>
> Guzzle from the geyser of instant gratification.
> Casual hookups
> Binge drinking
> Raucous parties
>
> Gulp at the fountain of materialism.
> Yachts
> Villas
> Planes
> Toys and trinkets
>
> Swig from the spring of success.
> Degrees
> Promotions
> Trophies
> Accolades aplenty

It's all sand. A mirage of meaning that will always leave you dying of thirst.

There is only one way to quench your thirsty soul. Drink the water that only Jesus offers. Here's His promise: "Anyone who drinks from My well will never be thirsty again. You will be an artesian spring with overflowing fountains that gush with joy and peace and endless life."

So churches have to decide: Are we going to build fences? Shall we obsess about certain behaviors and boundaries that define who's in and who's out? Or will we be a well-digging church? Shall we invite every person and say, "We would love to have you join us in this journey. Come! And be a part of a community where you will experience the love, acceptance, and forgiveness of Jesus."

I want to invite everybody I know to join my well-digging church, don't you?

How do we do this? Start with a question. Shift conversations to the spiritual. Share the benefits of faith. And offer unconditional acceptance.

It is my prayer that every one of us will be as effective at sharing Jesus as was this woman at the well. Oh, that our story would end in the same way as hers: "Many of the Samaritans from that town believed in him because of the woman's testimony" (John 4:39).

For reflection

1. Think about the quote, "Instead of focusing on thousands of converts, why not focus on being a good friend to one person?" Who is that "one person" God is calling you to befriend today?
2. Do you find it ironic that it was the church leaders who were most resistant to Jesus' ministry? Why or why not?
3. Jesus *had* to go through Samaria in order to meet a divine appointment with the woman at the well. Have you ever had a conversation with someone that you knew was divinely orchestrated? Share your stories in a small group.
4. Ellen White writes, "The hatred between Jews and Samaritans prevented the woman from offering a kindness to Jesus; but the Saviour was seeking to find the key to this heart, and with the tact born of divine love, He asked, not offered, a favor. The offer of a kindness might have been rejected; but trust awakens trust."[7] How might you nurture "tact born of divine love"? Share of ways you have found that illustrate how "trust awakens trust."
5. Do you tend to share your faith more with questions or answers? What are the advantages and disadvantages of each approach?
6. What are the benefits of being a disciple of Jesus?
7. Does your church tend to build fences to keep people in? Or do you offer "Living Water" that naturally attracts thirsty seekers? Which method do you prefer? Why?

---

1. Yurik Strasyuk, "9 Tips for Sharing Your Faith Without Being a Weirdo," *The Reluctant Skeptic* (blog), November 5, 2012, http://yuriystasyuk.com/9-tips-for-sharing-your-faith-without-being-a-weirdo/ (boldface and italics in the original).
2. Randy Newman, *Questioning Evangelism: Engaging People's Hearts the Way Jesus Did*, 2nd ed. (Grand Rapids, MI: Kregel Publications, 2004, 2017), 28.
3. Steve Corbett and Brian Fikkert, *When Helping Hurts: How to Alleviate Poverty Without Hurting the Poor . . . and Yourself* (Chicago: Moody Publishers, 2009, 2012), 127.
4. Corbett and Fikkert, *When Helping Hurts*, 127, 128.
5. Richard D. Phillips, *Jesus the Evangelist: Learning to Share the Gospel From the Book of John* (Lake Mary, FL: Reformation Trust, 2007), 115.
6. Des Cummings with Monica Reed, *CREATION Health Discovery* (Orlando, FL: Florida Hospital Publishing, 2005), 116.
7. Ellen G. White, *The Desire of Ages* (Mountain View, CA: Pacific Press®, 1940), 184.

PROFILES

Any method of evangelism will work—if God is in it.
—Leonard Ravenhill

"But I have raised you up for this very purpose, that I might show you my power and that my name might be proclaimed in all the earth."
—God, Exodus 9:16

If you ever feel like you aren't worthy enough, re member that Jesus used a bunch of flawed people to share hope to a flawed world.
—Jarrid Wilson

Chapter 5

AN EVANGELIST'S STORY: THE EXPERT WITNESS

Quick. Picture an evangelist.

OK, got it?

What came to mind? Did you think of a Bible-thumping man in a white suit who preaches with a southern accent? Or did you think of a mild-mannered statesman like Billy Graham or Ken Cox? Perhaps you envisioned a fire-faced street preacher with an accept-Jesus-right-now-or-I'll-beat-ya-black-n-blue attitude.

What I really wonder is this: Was the first evangelist that came to mind . . . you?

Bill Hybels laments that Christians often defer the task of evangelism to somebody else—anybody else. He writes,

> Many believers make a silent vow to themselves to just attend church, read their Bible, pray, enjoy fellowship, give some money, and serve in some capacity. They reason that the task of evangelism is better left in the hands of those whose personalities and temperments are cut out for "that kind of thing." They decide to let outgoing Extroverted Ed spread the Word. To have Dynamic Dave go out and save souls. To leave it to Soapbox Sally do her thing. "I'll be an usher," they say. "I'll have devotions. I'll help out with the children's choir, because I'm just not cut out to be an evangelist."

> This type of thinking is an all-out tragedy for the church. It's a tragedy for lost people.[1]

Ellen White agrees: "It is not merely the duty of the minister, but of every member of the church, to represent Christ to the world."[2] Don't panic. Jesus never asked you to be anyone other than yourself. He wants you to witness in the clothes you feel comfortable wearing. In this section, we will consider the stories of four exceptionally effective evangelists. The only thing they have in common is their uniqueness.

Let's start with the person most Bible scholars would name as the greatest evangelist in the Bible—Paul. What was it about the apostle that earned him such a lofty title? Of the many attributes we could spotlight, let's consider three.

1. His heart. First, Paul had a heart that would not stop beating for those far from God. Listen to his outcry on behalf of his own people.

> I have great sorrow and unceasing anguish in my heart. For I could wish that I myself were cursed and cut off from Christ for the sake of my people, those of my own race, the people of Israel. Theirs is the adoption to sonship; theirs the divine glory, the covenants, the receiving of the law, the temple worship and the promises. Theirs are the patriarchs, and from them is traced the human ancestry of the Messiah, who is God over all, forever praised! Amen (Romans 9:2–5).

Paul shares his "great sorrow and unceasing anguish." Why? For his brothers and sisters far from God. He is so passionate about this that he goes so far as to say, "I would give up my own eternal life for the sake of my people."

How I pray for this kind of heart, for myself and for my church.

It raises many questions: How much are we willing to sacrifice in order to reach lost people? What risks will we take? Are we willing to innovate? To think outside the bulletin? To join Paul and "become all things to all people so that by all possible means" (1 Corinthians 9:22) we might save some?

How far are we willing to go for the sake of the gospel?

Paul was willing to stretch any boundary short of compromising the gospel. We see this in the second attribute that makes him the poster child for evangelism. Notice how he adapts so fluidly, whatever the context.

2. His adaptability. "While Paul was waiting for them in Athens, he was greatly distressed to see that the city was full of idols" (Acts 17:16). Here again, we see a very troubled apostle because he sees idols littering the city and he knows this means one thing—a lot of folk in town don't know Jesus. "So he reasoned in the synagogue with both Jews and God-fearing Greeks, as well as in the marketplace day by day with those who happened to be there" (verse 17). Paul is multifaceted in his approach. First, he is an apologetics professor, reasoning with people in the synagogue. Next, he becomes a street preacher in the town square. From there, he engages in a debate with a "group of Epicurean and Stoic philosophers" (verse 18). Each setting requires a different evangelistic approach. So Paul has this "whatever it takes" mentality when it comes to sharing the gospel.

In any event, the message misses some of the people. In Paul's case, "Some of them asked, 'What is this babbler trying to say?' Others remarked, 'He seems to be advocating foreign gods.' They said this because Paul was preaching the good news about Jesus and the resurrection" (verse 18).

The point is, you need to be adaptable. The approach you use with your atheist neighbor will be different from what you say to your spiritually curious nephew.

The importance of adaptability was ingrained in me over the six summers I worked as a literature evangelist. Going door to door selling Bibles and Christian books was not the easiest of jobs, but it was rewarding beyond measure. Many of my church members today trace their conversion back to a literature evangelist who knocked on the door.

One day I was training a young woman who had joined our student team of colporteurs. We were invited into a home where the guy was clearly interested in purchasing our books. "I really, really want the books," he said, "but the problem is I can't afford them right now. I'm a farmer, and my only payday comes at harvest time. If you can come back in two months, I promise that I will buy the entire set."

"Not a problem at all," I said. "We have a payment plan known as the Farmer's Plan. Sounds like this will be perfect for you."

The trainee shot me a confused look. Then she interrupted, "We don't have a plan like that!"

I tried to gesture to her, "Shush! Be quiet already!"

"Here is how the plan works," I said to the farmer. "You put down a small deposit today, and then anytime over the next ninety days you can pay it off. No interest, same as cash. See, this gives farmers time to sell their crops and pay for the books after harvest."

He beamed. "That's perfect for me!" He purchased every book in our library.

When we got into the car, the student asked, "Why didn't they teach us about the Farmer's Plan in our training? I have never heard of that financing option."

"It's the same plan as the 90 Days Same as Cash."

"Right," she said. "But why did you call it the Farmer's Plan?"

"Because he is a farmer!"

Effective evangelists understand the importance of being flexible and making the gospel personal.

3. His focus. The final attribute that sets Paul apart as a soul winner is his focus. Historians tell us that Paul died about A.D. 64. His conversion happened about A.D. 34. So he had a thirty-year run of ministry. Right near the end of his life, we sense in Paul the same hot passion for lost people that we see shortly after his conversion.

In the sunset of his life, Paul writes to a young man named Timothy and says, "So do not be ashamed of the testimony about our Lord or of me his prisoner. Rather, join with me in suffering for the gospel, by the power of God" (2 Timothy 1:8). At the end of his life, Paul tells this young man, "Never be ashamed of the gospel. It is worth dying for." Then just before he dies, Paul reiterates this challenge. "But you, keep your head in all situations, endure hardship, do the work of an evangelist, discharge all the duties of your ministry" (2 Timothy 4:5). "Everything else you might do in ministry," Paul says, "pales in importance to the work of evangelism. Keep the main thing, the main thing."

Mind you, this is thirty years after Paul's conversion. After thirty years, this white-hot fire for souls is not typical. Bill Hybels, in his book *Just Walk Across the Room*, includes a graph that correlates the meaningful conversations Christians have with nonbelievers and the years the person has been a believer. The first year after committing to Jesus, the new believer will have twenty meaningful exchanges with people who are far from God. The second year after conversion that number drops to fifteen conversations with nonbelievers. In the third year, there are only seven such conversations. It continues to decline until year eight, when the number levels out to zero. In other words, after a person has been following Jesus for eight years, virtually all dialogue with unbelievers disappears.

Recently in my church after sharing this graphic, I asked people to raise their hands if they have been following Christ for eight years or longer. Nearly every hand went up. What followed was a sobering moment of silence. Without saying anything, we were confronted with the truth that unless churches are willing to be intentional about "the everyday commission," mission drift sets in and people drift toward self-care and narcissistic spirituality. Like Paul, we must never lose our focus.

Matthew Robert Payne reminds us:

> God has arranged it so that people have jobs in secular society among non-Christians because he wants you to share the flavor and aroma of Christ among people who don't smell that aroma. He wants you to share his love, his joy, his peace, his comfort and his understanding with people who are devoid of that. The Great Commission is a calling for us to go out and mix with the people of the world and demonstrate Jesus and his love and compassion to people in the world.[3]

Friends, this is our time, our calling. We must model the heart, the adaptability, and the focus of sharing Jesus. Let's break out of our holy enclaves and win this world for Jesus. Living as spiritual hermits won't help us in this mission.

Krish Kandiah tells of a woman who lived much of her life in isolation. Growing up in the United Kingdom, Kandiah and his family could always count on the next-door neighbor, Mrs. Oglive, to be around. She kept a spare key for the Kandiah's home in case they locked themselves out—which happened frequently.

Mrs. Oglive suffered from agoraphobia, the fear of open or public spaces. For forty years, she never ventured past her doorway. Dr. Kandiah writes,

> I can only imagine the heavy cloud of fear and frustration that surrounds her. Now frail and in the twilight of life, Mrs. Oglive's curtains are almost always drawn. But now and then, I still get locked out, and as she hands me the spare key, I am glad to see she is still alive.

> I see parallels between Mrs. Oglive and the contemporary church. Many Christians observe the world from behind closed curtains, bemoaning culture instead of engaging it. Many local churches are isolated from the wider community and world, . . . suffering from fear of an open public square with divergent viewpoints and lifestyles.[4]

From the public square to the synagogue to the street corner to the debate circle, Paul shows us what it looks like to overcome agoraphobia in the church. Every one of us is called to share Jesus—in our unique way, using our own style. We need not fear. For Jesus punctuates "the everyday commission" with this promise: "I am with you always, to the very end of the age" (Matthew 28:20).

For reflection

1. Complete this sentence: I am an expert at ________________ ________________.
2. Discuss different stereotypes people might have of evangelists. What is the best way to debunk misguided labels and ideas?
3. Fill in Ellen White's statement with your name. "It is not merely the duty of the minister, but of ____________________________, to represent Christ to the world." What is the best way for you to represent Christ to the world?
4. What are some specific ways in which God can make our hearts more sensitive toward people who don't know Jesus?
5. How open-minded are you to creative ideas of sharing the gospel? Discuss the potential upside and downside of trying new ways of reaching lost people.
6. Share your conversion story in a small group and tell how long you have been a follower of Jesus. Discuss the tendency we have to be less intentional about sharing Jesus with others the longer we have known Him. Would that be the case in your own story? What safeguards might help to address this issue?
7. Consider the statement, "Every one of us is called to share Jesus—in our unique way, using our own style." Describe "your way" and "your style" of sharing Jesus. Would your friends and family members agree with your assessment?

---

1. Bill Hybels with Kevin and Sherry Harney, *Reaching Out* (Grand Rapids, MI: Zondervan, 1996), 45, 46.

2. Ellen G. White, *Pastoral Ministry* (Silver Spring, MD: Ministerial Association of the General Conference of Seventh-day Adventists, 1995), 153.

3. Matthew Robert Payne, *Influencing Your World for Christ: Practical Everyday Evangelism* (Litchfield, IL: Revival Waves of Glory Books and Publishing, 2016), Kindle locs. 157–160.

4. Krish Kandiah, "An Explosion of Joy," *Christianity Today*, June 2014.

Chapter 6

A WHALE OF A STORY: THE RELUCTANT WITNESS

Two fishermen were swapping fish stories. As fishermen often do, the stories got bigger and better.

One fisherman said to the other, "Last summer in Montana, I caught a twenty-six-pound speckled trout."

"No way!" said the other fisherman. "Well the last time I was in Montana, I threw my bare hook in the water and caught a Coleman lantern."

"Really?"

"Oh yeah, and it was lit."

"No way!" the fisherman said.

"Yes, I'm telling you, it was still lit!"

Finally, the fisherman bargained, "Hey look, I'll take ten pounds off my trout if you'll blow out your lantern."

Such is the nature of fish stories, right? They get bigger and better until they are so good, they're unbelievable. Perhaps the most unbelievable fish story of all is that of Jonah, the reluctant witness. Of all the evangelists in the Bible, the one I relate to best would be this man who ran from God's calling. Let's take a look at the story.

> The word of the LORD came to Jonah son of Amittai: "Go to the great city of Nineveh and preach against it, because its wickedness has come up before me."

> But Jonah ran away from the LORD and headed for Tarshish. He went down to Joppa, where he found a ship bound for that port. After paying the fare, he went aboard and sailed for Tarshish to flee from the LORD (Jonah 1:1–3).

God calls Jonah to be an evangelist. In the same way, God calls every one of us to witness for Him.

Like Jonah, we are often reluctant to respond. Recently I asked my Facebook friends why we tend to be timid in sharing our faith. One word came up in nearly every reply: *fear*. Consider a few examples.

- "Fear of being asked a biblical question that I am unable to answer."
- "Fear of offending and fear of being rejected are at the top of my list."
- "Fear, afraid I will say the wrong thing or do the wrong thing, and/or feelings of not being worthy—that is, all my own sins make me hesitate."

Over and over this theme surfaced. In this sense, aren't we a lot like Jonah? God calls us to share Jesus with others, and we want to run the other direction.

Now in Jonah's case, his fear is understandable. Nineveh was an intimidating place. It had a wall that stretched around its eight-mile circumference that was fifty feet wide and one hundred feet high. Just the thought of it put fear in people.

The Ninevites were Assyrians. They were renowned for their cruelty. For example, one of the kings of Nineveh, Ashur-nasirpal II, wrote this about his conquests: "I slaughtered them; with their blood I dyed the mountain red like wool. . . . The heads of their warriors I cut off, and I formed them into a pillar over against their city; their young men and their maidens I burned in the fire! . . . I flayed all the chief men who had revolted, and I covered the pillar with their skins."[1] He literally skinned them alive.

Another leader of Assyria described what he did to his captive: "I pierced his chin with my keen hand dagger. Through his jaw . . . I passed a rope, put a dog chain upon him and made him occupy . . . a kennel."[2]

"Jonah, go to the great city of Nineveh and preach against it." That's like God calling you to go and evangelize ISIS terrorists. I understand why Jonah was reluctant. But why are we so afraid to share our faith?

Even though the stories may differ, we can still learn from Jonah. Of the twelve Minor Prophets in the Bible, this is the only one that is written in narrative form. Using that format, let's walk through the story in four scenes. In each scene, we find Jonah in a different position.

Scene one: On his back, sleeping

> Then the LORD sent a great wind on the sea, and such a violent storm arose that the ship threatened to break up. All the sailors were afraid and each cried out to his own god. And they threw the cargo into the sea to lighten the ship.
>
> But Jonah had gone below deck, where he lay down and fell into a deep sleep (Jonah 1:4, 5).

In this first scene, we find Jonah in the most unusual position—on his back, sleeping. But God will not let him sleep through the storm. When God calls you, He's serious about your obedience.

Perhaps you've silenced God's calling to witness to someone at work or in your neighborhood or in your family. You've resisted the prompting of the Holy Spirit. You've been blubbering excuses as to why you can't get off your backside and do what God is calling you to do.

Lois Chaney, in the book *God Is No Fool,* writes:

> Moses said, "Oh come on now! Be sensible! Not me! I'm a terrible speaker. They'd never listen to me." And God said, "Oh, for crying out loud! O.K., I'll use your brother to help with the speaking." And Moses led God's people out of disintegration.
>
> Jonah said, "Oh come on now! Be sensible! Not me! I'm not the type." And after a rather unexpected vacation in a fish, just thinking things over, he talked to God's people, and led them God's way.
>
> And Zacharias said, "Oh come on now! Be sensible! Not me! My wife and I are too old to have kids." And God said, "Oh shut up!" And he did shut up—for nine months. And John was born, and the way for the Christ was opened up.

> And I heard a child say, "I can't serve God, I'm too young."
> And I heard a boy say, "I can't serve God, I'm not good enough."
> And I heard a woman say, "I can't serve God, I'm not skilled enough."
> I wonder if God ever gets any new problems.[3]

Young or old, educated or not, like Jonah, God is calling every one of us to witness for Him. In this case, God will not let Jonah rest. He sends a great storm. The sailors heave Jonah overboard. The storm subsides.

All this drama makes for a memorable evangelistic campaign! It worked. Verse 16 records, "At this the men greatly feared the LORD, and they offered a sacrifice to the LORD and made vows to him."

The story continues, "When Jonah fell into the sea, the LORD chose a very big fish to swallow Jonah. He was in the stomach of the fish for three days and three nights" (verse 17, ERV).

Scene two: On his knees, praying

For our next scene, we move to the inside of this very big fish. We find our reluctant witness on his knees, praying.

> From inside the fish Jonah prayed to the LORD his God. He said:
>
> "In my distress I called to the LORD,
> and he answered me.
> From deep in the realm of the dead I called for help,
> and you listened to my cry" (Jonah 2:1, 2).

The chapter concludes, "The LORD commanded the fish, and it vomited Jonah onto dry land" (verse 10).

Many years ago, my brother ate fish at a company banquet. He got food poisoning and ended up in the hospital. He has not touched a piece of fish since. So I have heard of a man getting sick from eating fish, but in this story, the fish gets sick from eating a man. God intervenes, and the fish vomits Jonah onto dry land.

We are reminded in this story that even in all of our reluctance and rebellion, God hears and answers prayer. God intervenes on Jonah's behalf and commands the fish to burp up his cargo. God delivers, even in the worst of storms.

Years ago, I clipped an article from the *Seattle Times* that helps to illustrate this. In 1972, Lynn Ray Collins was hit by a drunk driver. He spent the next eleven months in a coma teetering on the frail line between life and death. Finally, he recovered, but he could not speak. Doctors said he would never speak again.

Collins was grateful just to be alive. For most of his life he communicated by sign language and the computer. More recently, Lynn Ray Collins sustained another serious injury. He was walking on a sidewalk when a driver swerved out of control and sent him flying into the glass window of a department store. When Collins regained consciousness, to his utter surprise and shock, he could speak.

Dr. Raymond Ufford, Collins's longtime doctor, was baffled. He couldn't explain what happened.

Well that's the good news from the book of Jonah. God can bring good even out of terrible storms. Perhaps you are in a storm right now. Maybe you feel swallowed by darkness—like you're in the belly of a fish. Don't despair. Get on your knees. The God of Jonah, who commands the wind and the rain and fish, is still in control!

God can get you on your feet again. He can set you on the right road.

Scene three: On his feet, preaching

Next, we find Jonah on his feet. Chapter 3 describes our third scene. Jonah preaches a sermon that consists of only five Hebrew words, translated, "After 40 days, Nineveh will be destroyed!" (Jonah 3:4, ERV).

This is a no-nonsense, in-your-face sermon. The response to Jonah's terse, incisive message was astounding.

> The people of Nineveh believed God. They decided to stop eating for a time to think about their sins. They put on special clothes to show they were sorry. All the people in the city did this, from the most important to the least important.
>
> When the king of Nineveh heard about this, he left his throne, removed his robe, put on special clothes to show that he was sorry, and sat in ashes (verses 5, 6, ERV).

Talk about extraordinary results from an evangelistic series! I can't help but wonder what miracles we'd see if we trusted God enough to witness whenever and however He calls us. Sadly, I have a lot of Jonah in me, and I'm inclined to escape to Tarshish rather than going to Nineveh.

I think of the weekend I spoke for an event at Columbia University in New York City. Noticing the afternoon was slated as "Witnessing to Our City," I asked one of the organizers what that was about.

"We are going to Grand Central Station to witness," she said. "It will be tons of fun."

"Fun" wasn't the word that came to my mind. *Dread*, *awkwardness*, *fear*, and a bunch of other words—yes, but *fun* was not among them. But it's usually not advisable to preach all weekend about following Jesus and then bail when it comes to the "follow" part.

So I jumped on the subway with the eager evangelists, and we were off on our adventure. The plan was to approach waiting riders and ask if they could use a prayer.

"Yes! I definitely need prayer," the first woman said. "My dad has kidney failure, and it doesn't look good. Would you pray for him?"

"I would love to," I said. And I meant it.

Not once did someone decline my offer. Which makes me wonder if my angst over witnessing is a lot of fear over nothing. If God can take care of Jonah preaching to terrorists, surely he's got my back in the Big Apple—or wherever He needs me to go.

Back to Jonah: Even after God pulls off the unlikeliest miracle and the terrorists are saved, Jonah sulks because things didn't play out as he had threatened. In the fourth and final scene, we find a pouting prophet whining to God.

Scene four: On his face, pouting

> But to Jonah this seemed very wrong, and he became angry. He prayed to the Lord, "Isn't this what I said, Lord, when I was still at home? That is what I tried to forestall by fleeing to Tarshish. I knew that you are a gracious and compassionate God, slow to anger and abounding in love, a God who relents from sending calamity. Now, Lord, take away my life, for it is better for me to die than to live" (Jonah 4:1–3).

Poor Jonah—pulsating veins popping from his crimson neck. Pointing his bony finger at God, he said, "I knew You didn't have the guts to follow through. That's exactly why I never wanted this witnessing gig in the first place. I make an idiot out of myself for You, and then You back out on me. Just let me die, would You?"

Remember, this is the same prophet that cried out in desperation for God to save him from the fish. God showed compassion and gave him a second chance. But now Jonah would rather die than give Nineveh a second chance.

How quickly we forget the grace extended to us, as we demand justice for others! I think of the time I tweeted into a national radio show commenting on the big news story of the morning. New York Yankees first baseman, Mark Teixeira, made very disparaging, public comments about an umpire who supposedly missed a close call and cost the Yankees a win. I weighed in with a tweet: "Teixeira wasn't complaining when his teammate D. Wise pretended to catch a foul ball. Yanks got the out & the win—but shouldn't have."

The radio host read my tweet and commented, "Yes! Karl Haffner makes a great point. We never heard Teixeira sniveling about that miscall, did we?" So Teixeira was griping about a controversial call that could have gone either way and yet said nothing about the game a few days prior in which the Yankees left fielder DeWayne Wise dove into the stands and pretended to have the ball. The umpire never asked to see proof of the catch! Meanwhile, a fan held up the ball.

It's not just Teixeira or Jonah that thinks this way. We all do, don't we? Whether we are preaching or hearing about grace, we all need it.

So be faithful when God calls you to share His grace. Do not fear. Do not run. Do not judge. Do not whine. In other words, don't be a Jonah. When you commit to be a fisher of people, God will give you the greatest fish stories of all.

For reflection

1. In your opinion, why are Christians often reluctant to share their faith?
2. What is the most difficult thing God has called you to do? What part of Jonah's story do you relate to the most?
3. Have you ever made excuses to God when you sense Him calling you to do something? When it comes to answering God's call, whom do you most identify with in the Bible? Moses? Jonah? Zacharias? Elijah? Peter? And why?
4. Share with your small group a difficult storm you have been through. What did you learn about yourself in that experience? What did you learn about God through it?
5. Was there ever a time when someone gave you a second chance that you didn't deserve? What impact did that have on you? How can you extend the grace you received from God to others?
6. Reflect on the insight of Ellen White: "God's messengers in the great cities are not to become discouraged over the wickedness, the injustice, the depravity, which they are called upon to face while endeavoring to proclaim the glad tidings of salvation. The Lord would cheer every such worker with the same message that He gave to the apostle Paul in wicked Corinth: 'Be not afraid, but speak, and hold not thy peace: for I am with thee, and no man shall set on thee to hurt thee: for I have much people in this city.' "[4]
7. Identify the primary lesson you learn from Jonah when it comes to being an effective witness for God.

---

1. James E. Smith, *The Minor Prophets* (Joplin, MO: College Press, 2006), 102.
2. John Mark Conner, *God Has a Name* (Grand Rapids, MI: Zondervan, 2017).
3. Lois Chaney, *God Is No Fool* (Nashville, TN: Abingdon Press, 1969), 130, 131.
4. Ellen G. White, *Prophets and Kings* (Mountain View, CA: Pacific Press®, 1917), 277.

Chapter 7

A DEVIL OF A STORY: THE PERSONAL WITNESS

Second Timothy 4:5 states bluntly, "Do the work of an evangelist." As Christians, we know that we're *supposed* to share our faith; but it often feels awkward, doesn't it?

Pulitzer Prize–winning author Annie Dillard tells of her neighbor's awkward attempts to witness. Living in rural Virginia, she went to meet her new neighbor. The woman was polite but nervous. Dillard writes,

> She did not let me go; she was worried about something else. She worked her hands. I waited on the other side of the screen door until she came out with it:
>
> "Do you know the Lord as your personal savior?"
>
> My heart went out to her. No wonder she had been so nervous. She must have to ask this of everyone, absolutely everyone, she meets. That is Christian witness. . . . I wanted to make her as happy as possible, reward her courage, and run.[1]

Perhaps you can relate to Dillard's story. You have experienced both sides of that screen door. You know the Bible commands us to do the work of an evangelist. But when you try, you're way outside your comfort zone. If you can relate, take heart. There is an evangelist in Scripture you have to meet.

Jesus was intent on meeting this man. So He said to His disciples, "Let us go over to the other side" (Mark 4:35).[2] This is similar to the story of Jesus needing to go through Samaria (see John 4:4). In this case, "the other side" of the lake referred to more than geography. Jesus was suggesting they go from the region of Galilee across the Sea of Galilee into the Decapolis region. In Greek, "Decapolis" means "ten cities." This was enemy territory. Only pagan people lived in the Decapolis.

In Jesus' day, the Jews followed a tradition. Joshua 3:10 contains the promise that God "will certainly drive out before you the Canaanites, Hittites, Hivites, Perizzites, Girgashites, Amorites and Jebusites"—also called "the seven nations of Canaan." Acts 13:19 records the fulfillment of that promise: God "overthrew seven nations in Canaan, giving their land to his people as their inheritance."

According to the rabbinic tradition, the seven nations of Canaan settled in the Decapolis region. So the area was populated with pagan temples, ruins of which are still being excavated today. Cults abounded, exalting sexuality, violence, and greed.

Decapolis was also a center for Roman power. Six thousand Roman soldiers were stationed on "the other side." The legion's symbol was a pig's head. Pigs were worshiped—which, of course, was highly offensive to all Israelites. Moreover, the Jews regarded "the other side" as Satan's hometown. It was dark and demonic. It was the place all Jewish rabbis avoided—well, except for Jesus.

Phillip Yancey comments on the *Message* paraphrase that renders John 1:14 to say that "the Word became flesh and blood, and moved into the neighborhood." But you see, the "neighborhood" that John is talking about was "the other side." Here's how Yancey describes it:

> A succession of great empires tramped through the territory of Israel as if wiping their feet on the vaunted promised land. After the Assyrians and Babylonians came the Persians, who were in turn defeated by Alexander the Great. [Alexander was eventually followed by] Antiochus IV Epiphanes, the Jews' [worst] villain until Hitler.
>
> . . . Antiochus began waging war against the Jewish religion. He transformed the temple of God into a worship center for Zeus and proclaimed himself God incarnate. He forced young boys to undergo reverse circumcision operations and flogged an aged priest

> to death for refusing to eat pork. In one of his most notorious acts, he sacrificed an unclean pig on the altar in the Most Holy Place, smearing its blood around the temple sanctuary.
>
> Antiochus's actions so incensed the Jews that they rose up in an armed revolt led by the Maccabeans. . . . Their victory was short-lived. Before long, Roman legions marched into Palestine to quash the rebellion. . . . After the Roman conquest, nearly the entire land lay in ruins. . . .
>
> This, then, was the neighborhood Jesus moved into: a sinister place with a somber past and a fearful future.[3]

Not only did Jesus move into the neighborhood, but He also insisted on frequenting the sketchiest places—such as "the hood" on the other side.

Here's what awaited Jesus on the other side:

> They went across the lake to the region of the Gerasenes. When Jesus got out of the boat, a man with an impure spirit came from the tombs to meet him. This man lived in the tombs, and no one could bind him anymore, not even with a chain. For he had often been chained hand and foot, but he tore the chains apart and broke the irons on his feet. No one was strong enough to subdue him. Night and day among the tombs and in the hills he would cry out and cut himself with stones.
>
> When he saw Jesus from a distance, he ran and fell on his knees in front of him. He shouted at the top of his voice, "What do you want with me, Jesus, Son of the Most High God? In God's name don't torture me!" For Jesus had said to him, "Come out of this man, you impure spirit!" (Mark 5:1–8).

William Barclay claims that we cannot begin to understand this story unless we see how serious a case of demon-possession this was. It's worth noting that Jesus made more than one attempt to heal him. Jesus began with his usual method—an authoritative order for the demon to come out. This didn't work. So Jesus asked the demon's name because rabbis taught that if the identity was known, the demon's power was broken.

" 'My name is Legion,' he replied, 'for we are many.' And he begged

Jesus again and again not to send them out of the area" (verses 9, 10).

Legion is a loaded word. This story is full of loaded words. There's a legion of Roman soldiers who live there. It is a reminder of all the powers that oppose Jesus.

"A large herd of pigs was feeding on the nearby hillside. The demons begged Jesus, 'Send us among the pigs; allow us to go into them.' He gave them permission, and the impure spirits came out and went into the pigs. The herd, about two thousand in number, rushed down the steep bank into the lake and were drowned" (verses 11–13).

For the ancient Jews, nothing was more repulsive than a pig. It's much different today. We think of pigs as cute. Who doesn't love Porky Pig? Or do you remember the old TV show, *Green Acres,* that featured a pet pig named Arnold Ziffel? I have friends who used to have a pig they named Stripples (after the vegetarian bacon product). They claimed Stripples was the best pet they ever had. In Jesus' day, pigs were never beloved pets.

"Those tending the pigs ran off and reported this in the town and countryside, and the people went out to see what had happened" (verse 14).

The scene was quite the spectacle. Imagine being a pig herder and your boss wants to know, "What happened to all my pigs?" You explain, "They committed mass suicide." That's a tough sell.

"When they came to Jesus, they saw the man who had been possessed by the legion of demons, sitting there, dressed and in his right mind; and they were afraid" (verse 15).

It's interesting to notice the healing, calming effect of Jesus. This wild, naked madman was transformed into a sane and sensible citizen. Jesus can still have that effect on people.

The students from our local church school witnessed this calming effect the Christmas of 2016 when they were on a choir trip to Chicago. They were on a public bus when a man became very aggressive and contentious toward the students and sponsors. He accused one of the sponsors of being a terrorist—which is not something to be taken lightly. This man clearly had mental health issues, as he became more threatening and confrontational.

"The situation could have easily escalated," writes the principal Darren Wilkins. Instead, a miracle happened. Another sponsor quietly suggested the students sing. They did, timidly at first, and then from the diaphragm. The beautiful sounds of Christmas filled the bus. The tormentor was annoyed, then resigned, then moved to tears. The final note triggered applause throughout the bus. Spontaneously the choir struck up "O Holy Night." It sounded like a bus full of angels weaving through the dark streets of Chicago. Song after song washed over the passengers. The angry one forgot his rage and absorbed the news of peace on Earth, good will to men.[4]

Jesus has a calming effect on both tormentors and the tormented. But for those observing the man, the Bible says "they were afraid" (verse 15). "Those who had seen it told the people what had happened to the demon-possessed man—and told about the pigs as well. Then the people began to plead with Jesus to leave their region" (verses 16, 17).

Funny how the people do not respond by saying, "Wow, this is a man of great power!" They don't think, *This man could heal my sick child.* Or, *I need to follow this guy and let him change me.*

Instead, they begged Jesus to leave. After all, He's from the other side.

Somebody from the other side can't be trusted. Somebody from the other side comes only to condemn. Somebody from the other side is evil.

They fear anybody from the other side.

All the locals fear Jesus. Well, except for the one formerly crazed demoniac. "As Jesus was getting into the boat, the man who had been demon-possessed begged to go with him" (verse 18).

This man prostrates himself before Jesus: "I've been living in darkness all my life, and it has destroyed me. Let me leave here. I just want to be with You. I'll leave everybody, all my possessions—which isn't much—to follow You." He doesn't just make a request; he begs, he cries, he is desperate.

And Jesus says, "No. Stay here. Tell your story."

Imagine the man's feeling when the boat rows away and he's not in it. But he says to himself, *I will do what He said. He saved my life. Since He asked me to tell other people about Him, that's exactly what I'll do.*

"So the man went away and began to tell in the Decapolis how much Jesus had done for him. And all the people were amazed" (verse 20).

When Jesus goes over to the other side the first time, just one pathetic, demon-tormented wretch meets him. On the second trip to the Decapolis, Jesus arrived and "great crowds came to him, bringing the lame, the blind, the crippled, the mute and many others, and laid them at his feet; and he healed them. The people were amazed when they saw the mute speaking, the crippled made well, the lame walking and the blind seeing. And they praised the God of Israel" (Matthew 15:30, 31).

On His second trip, Jesus received a wildly enthusiastic reception. What happened? Well, one man decided he would do the work of an evangelist. Apparently, he wasn't intimated by this calling to evangelism. He didn't take a pass on "the everyday commission" that Jesus gave him for fear of feeling awkward or rejected.

Instead, he simply told others what Jesus meant to him. And in that simple act of obedience, he changed the world.

Jesus is calling us to do the same. Do the work of an evangelist.

For reflection

1. When you read the blunt command of Paul, "Do the work of an evangelist," how do you feel?

    a. Guilty
    b. Excited
    c. Scared
    d. Ambivalent
    e. Ready
    f. All of the above
    g. None of the above. I feel ____________________.
    Explain.

2. In your world today, what represents "the other side" where Christians are often reticent to go?
3. What does the story of the demoniac teach us about sharing our faith?
4. What similarities do you see between Decapolis and the culture today?
5. Reflect on the following commentary of Ellen White. How can her insights provide hope when sharing your faith?

    > In causing the destruction of the swine, it was Satan's purpose to turn the people away from the Saviour, and prevent the preaching of the gospel in that region. But this very occurrence roused the whole country as nothing else could have done, and directed attention to Christ. Though the Saviour Himself departed, the men whom He had healed remained as witnesses to His power. Those who had been mediums of the prince of darkness became channels of light, messengers of the Son of God. Men marveled as they listened to the wondrous news. A door was opened to the gospel throughout that region.[5]

6. Suppose God moved into your neighborhood through you. What might that look like?

7. How would you answer a friend who asks, "What has Jesus done for you?"

---

1. Annie Dillard, *Teaching a Stone to Talk* (New York: Harper Perennial, 2013), 98.

2. Much of the commentary for this story was inspired by a downloaded transcript of John Ortberg's sermon "Jesus Hits the Road," preached August 2, 2006, http://www.willowcreek.com.

3. Philip Yancey, *The Question That Never Goes Away* (Grand Rapids, MI: Zondervan, 2013), 87, 88.

4. Darren Wilkins, "Miracle on a Bus," *Visitor*, March 2016, 34.

5. White, *The Desire of Ages*, 340.

Chapter 8

A VOLUNTEER'S STORY: SERVING AS A WITNESS

Her name caught my attention: Lynette LeGette. Great name, right? I also loved her story as published in *The Southeast Outlook.*

Lynette learned of 21,800 patients each year who would receive chemotherapy treatments in her hometown of Louisville, Kentucky. It occurred to her, "I can do something to help these patients." She thought of how many of them would lose their hair. She learned that patients complain about being cold during the night and wrap pajamas or towels around their heads to keep warm. That's when she decided to make hats that she could give away. She said, "I thought I couldn't possibly meet that need. It seemed an overwhelming project."

Lynette recruited six volunteers and over the course of a couple years made a thousand turbans and hats they provided at no charge for women in need. One patient received several of Lynette's hats. Later, Lynette met that woman's seven-year-old daughter. The kid wrapped her arms around Lynette's legs and said, "You made my mom so happy! Because of you she has a hat to go with every outfit."

Lynette became known as the "Hat Lady." Her other nickname was "the modern-day Dorcas." She says, "When you ask the Lord what you should do, you need to be willing to listen for the direction and recognize the opportunities he gives you."[1]

Indeed, God will provide you many opportunities to be an evangelist.

You may not think of Lynette, "the modern-day Dorcas," or the real Dorcas in Scripture as evangelists. But both women had major evangelistic impact.

The original story of Dorcas starts in Acts 9:36. "In Joppa there was a disciple named Tabitha (in Greek her name is Dorcas)." Just the fact that her name is given in two different languages suggests a connection she made between two different factions of the ancient church, the Hellenists and the Hebrews.

This is what we know about Dorcas: "She was always doing good and helping the poor" (verse 36). That's a very complimentary legacy, isn't it? I would sure be happy to be remembered as the person who was always "doing good and helping the poor," wouldn't you?

"About that time she became sick and died, and her body was washed and placed in an upstairs room" (verse 37). Luke provides the details of how they prepared her corpse. He did not want skeptics suggesting that maybe Dorcas was not really dead.

The story continues:

> Lydda was near Joppa; so when the disciples heard that Peter was in Lydda, they sent two men to him and urged him, "Please come at once!"
>
> Peter went with them, and when he arrived he was taken upstairs to the room. All the widows stood around him, crying and showing him the robes and other clothing that Dorcas had made while she was still with them. (verses 38, 39).

Luke gives special attention to women, especially widows. In his Gospel, he mentions widows nine times; in the book of Acts, three times.

"Peter sent them all out of the room; then he got down on his knees and prayed" (verse 40). Once again, we are reminded of the source of power for the early Christian church. Prayer remains central to all the miracle stories in Scripture. Without prayer, our churches are powerless to grow.

"Turning toward the dead woman, he said, 'Tabitha, get up.' She opened her eyes, and seeing Peter she sat up. He took her by the hand and helped her to her feet. Then he called for the believers, especially the widows, and presented her to them alive. This became known all over

Joppa, and many people believed in the Lord" (verses 40–42).

Amazing, isn't it? Not just the healing part of the story, but the evangelistic impact a life of simple service can have. Because of one evangelist who sought to serve, "many people" came into a saving relationship with Jesus.

N. T. Wright observes:

> Do not belittle the ministry of stitching, sewing, knitting and generally providing for the needs of the larger community—especially at a time before anyone dreamed of mass-produced clothes. And do not forget to celebrate, as Luke does here, the fact that the apparently ordinary people are not ordinary to God, and that when we tell the story of the great sweep of God's purposes in history there are, at every point, . . . the Dorcases who smile out of the page at us, like the robin in the garden, and remind us what it's really all about.[2]

For the past ten years, I've enjoyed a front-row seat to observe one of the fastest growing churches in America. Over thirty years ago, Steve Sjogren started the Cincinnati Vineyard Church in a barn used for square dancing with a group of thirty-seven people. By the second week, attendance dropped to twenty. The church has never wavered from its original calling to show God's love in practical ways. Some of the ways they have practiced the work of Dorcas include giving away bottles of water at busy stoplights, one-dollar carwashes where drivers are given money for the privilege of serving them in Jesus' name, delivering free food door-to-door, and even cleaning toilets for local businesses. Thousands of people are served every month who have spiritual, emotional, and physical needs.

In his book *Conspiracy of Kindness*, Pastor Sjogren tells the true story of Joe Delaney and his eight-year-old son, Jared, who were playing catch in their backyard.

> Jared asked, "Dad, is there a God?"
>
> Joe replied that he went to church only a few times when he was a kid; he really had no idea.
>
> Jared ran into the house. "I'll be right back!" he yelled.
>
> Moments later he returned with a helium balloon from the circus, a pen, and an index card. "I'm going to send God an airmail message," Jared explained. "Dear God," he wrote, "if you are real,

and you are there, send people who know you to Dad and me."

God, I hope you're watching, Joe thought, as they watched the balloon and message sail away.

Two days later, Joe and Jared pulled into a car wash sponsored by the Sjogren's church. When Joe asked, "How much?" Sjogren answered, "It's free. No strings attached. We just want to show God's love in a practical way."

"Are you guys Christians, the kind of Christians who believe in God?" Joe asked.

Sjogren said, "Yes, we're that kind of Christians." From that encounter, Steve led Joe to faith in Christ.[3]

Who knows? Many people may be one act of kindness from meeting a true Christian. God is looking for more modern-day Dorcases. Why not answer His call today?

For reflection

1. Who first comes to mind when you think of a "servant leader"? Why?
2. How does Dorcas's legacy make you feel: "She was always doing good and helping the poor"? What do you hope for your legacy to be?
3. React with a small group to the statement, "Ordinary people are not ordinary to God." What might this suggest in terms of how God wants to use you to build His kingdom?
4. How would you respond to the Christian who says, "I don't preach at people or tell them what to believe. They will accept Christ just by watching me serve others"? Do you think there is a danger in the Dorcas approach to witnessing by putting the onus on seekers to explore the gospel solely from observing your acts of service? Why or why not?
5. Consider the statement, "Without prayer, our churches are powerless to grow." How can you elevate the importance of prayer in your life? What can you do to help create and/or protect a culture of prayer in your church?
6. How can you show God's love in practical ways this week?
7. Of the different evangelists profiled in this book—Paul, Jonah, the demoniac, and Dorcas—which one do you relate to the most and why?

---

1. *The Southeast Outlook*, December 16, 2004; submitted by Van Morris, Mt. Washington, Kentucky, from http://www.preachingtoday.com/illustrations/2005/may/15900.html (accessed July 17, 2017).

2. N. T. Wright, *Acts for Everyone, Part 1: Chapters 1–12* (London: Society for Promoting Christian Knowledge, 2008), 155.

3. Retold by Tom Lundeen in *Fresh Illustrations for Preaching & Teaching From Leadership Journal*, ed. Edward K. Rowell (Grand Rapids, MI: Baker, 1997), quoted in "How to Meet a Christian," PreachingToday.com, accessed November 29, 2017, http://www.preachingtoday.com/illustrations/1998/february/3627.html.

PARABLES

God had an only Son,
and he made him a missionary.
—David Livingstone

Jesus always used stories and illustrations like these when speaking to the crowds. In fact, he never spoke to them without using such parables.
—Matthew 13:34, NLT

To every lost soul, Christ says: Come unto Me. To every redeemed soul, Christ says: Go for Me.
—Unknown

Chapter 9

THE SOWER AND THE SEED

Matthew 13:1–23

MustardSeedThoughts.com posts this parable:

> A teacher cultivated his lessons, having adapted the information that was necessary for knowledge, wisdom, and success. He spoke passionately and without exception to his classes, regardless of the reception he received. Some of his lessons fell on deaf ears, where students were allowed to sleep in the back of class, and others chose to be distracted by their cellphones and laptops. Others appeared intent on listening, but failed to truly engage the material, as their purpose there was driven solely by their parents' wishes. When springtime came, they quickly found other distractions, and failed to continue coming to class. Some of the students longed to listen and to learn, but their relationships with certain other students caused them to become distracted, to ignore their studies, and to skip class when they were encouraged to do so. But some of the lessons were heard by the ears of receptive students, who worked hard, sought additional help, and continued to prosper in school, and life, grasping the opportunities presented to them.[1]

The story, of course, is based on a well-known parable that Jesus told. This was the first of seven parables in Matthew 13 where Jesus hammers home the familiar theme of expanding His kingdom; that is, seeking and saving the lost. In a book about sharing Jesus, don't you think it only makes sense to consult Jesus Himself on how we ought to do this?

This first parable goes like this:

> "A farmer went out to sow his seed. As he was scattering the seed, some fell along the path, and the birds came and ate it up. Some fell on rocky places, where it did not have much soil. It sprang up quickly, because the soil was shallow. But when the sun came up, the plants were scorched, and they withered because they had no root. Other seed fell among thorns, which grew up and choked the plants. Still other seed fell on good soil, where it produced a crop—a hundred, sixty or thirty times what was sown. Whoever has ears, let them hear" (Matthew 13:3–9).

Let me share a couple of panoramic observations about this story on growth. First, growth is God's intention for His kingdom and all His children. Growth is normal. It is a sign of health. When anything alive is healthy, it grows. To be alive is to have the capacity for growth.

When our daughter was born, I was struck by the amazing rate of her growth. When we left the hospital, she weighed about six pounds, a tiny little thing. She ate and ate and ate. By the end of her first year, she weighed slightly over eighteen pounds. She tripled her weight in one year, which is common for babies. If she kept tripling every year, by the time she was four years old, she would have weighed 486 pounds!

Growth is a normal sign of a healthy life. Conversely, when you stop growing, you start dying. There's no greater tragedy than stagnation. Doctors refer to a condition where babies do not grow as FTT, which means "failure to thrive." Thriving is normal. When it doesn't happen, professionals will go to great lengths to remedy the situation.

Similarly, in churches, thriving is what we are supposed to do. When growth doesn't happen, we ought to go to great lengths to remove the barriers preventing it.

Recently, I visited the fastest-growing church in my hometown of Dayton, Ohio. The senior pastor shared, "When I planted this church twenty-five years ago, I did so with a philosophy I gleaned from a book on church growth. The principle is this: All healthy organisms grow. So I figured if our church is healthy, it will always grow. I've always defined my job, then, as removing all obstacles to growth so our church can do what all healthy organisms are designed to do."

He elaborated on some of the obstacles they had to remove through the years that prevented growth. Inadequate parking spaces, children's rooms that were overcrowded, church members who were divisive—to mention just a few barriers. His observation continues to shape my thinking as we pray for God to grow our church. If we are healthy, we will grow. So ask yourself, What things might be stunting that growth?

This leads to the second observation: We don't make growth happen.

I think of the football player David Pollack, who played defensive end for the University of Georgia. Although a very successful defensive player, Pollack was listed in scouting reports from the National Football League as being somewhat short for playing as a defensive lineman. When asked about his height in an interview, Pollack quipped, "I've been sleeping upside down. It's not working."[2]

You cannot make yourself grow. This principle rings true for churches as well. In my local church, we have two hundred prayer warriors who pray daily that we would see growth in our church. But we all recognize that only God can make the church grow. We must rely fully on God for growth, partnering with Him by removing any obstacles to growth. In the words of Rick Warren, "Church growth is a partnership between God and man. Churches grow by the power of God through the skilled effort of people."[3]

Back to Jesus' story; notice there are three elements: the seed, the sower, and the soil. Two of them are constant and one is variable.

The seed doesn't change. This is not a story about good seeds and bad seeds. The seed, the Word of God, the kingdom of heaven, the good news—the seed is a constant that will always bear fruit if you put it in the right environment.

The second constant is the sower. This is not a story about good sowers and bad sowers. One of the interesting nuances to the story is how generous the sower is with his seed. In fact, he is extravagant. He doesn't seem to be real conscientious about where the seed lands.

The sower doesn't change. The seed doesn't change. So what's the variable? It's the soil!

Whether the seed survives and flourishes or fails to thrive and dies, it all depends on the soil. You can count on the seed. You can count on the sower. Everything hinges on the soil, and the soil, of course, represents you and me.

Growth is normal. It's a gift. It comes from God. We cannot make it happen; but there are barriers—that is, certain soil conditions—that can prevent growth.

So let's do some soil analysis, shall we? Consider the four conditions of soil that Jesus unpacks later in the chapter.

1. Path. First, Jesus speaks to the packed-down dirt of the pathway. "Listen then to what the parable of the sower means: When anyone hears the message about the kingdom and does not understand it, the evil one comes and snatches away what was sown in their heart. This is the seed sown along the path" (Matthew 13:18, 19).

In Israel, the soil conditions were dry anyway, but if the seed fell on a hard-packed, well-traveled path, it didn't have a chance to grow. So Jesus is illustrating here that growth requires soil that is soft.

Jesus knows how it goes with some people. Hearts can become hard toward God. Bitterness, cynicism, and anger can squelch the Spirit.

In the same way, churches can become hard-hearted rather than humble and pliable. So how would you assess the heart condition of your church? Are members open-minded to change? To risk-taking? To innovative methods of sowing seeds?

Interestingly, this is the reason why Jesus spoke in parables to the church of His day—because people are hard-hearted. Defensive. Shielded with a protective coating.

In between this story and its explanation, the disciples ask Jesus, "Why do you speak to the people in parables?" (verse 10). Jesus cites Isaiah, "Though seeing, they do not see; though hearing, they do not hear or understand" (Matthew 13:13). In other words, people resist truth. They can see, but they don't want to see, so they don't. They can hear, but they don't want to hear, so they don't. They're guarded. Their hearts are calloused to truth. So how did Jesus get past their defenses? He told parables.

In the Greek, the word *parable* is *paraballein.* It's a compound word taken from two words. *Ballein* means to throw, and *para* means alongside of—"to throw alongside of." The idea is that Jesus would take an occurrence or picture from everyday life and throw it alongside a truth about the kingdom of God.

In Hebrew, the word for "parable" is *machal*—which is a broad word. It means a riddle or a puzzle, something you have to think about. There's a role that you have to play in understanding it. There will often be a twist in the story as well.

This brings to mind the story of the boy with a learning disability who was approached by a conman who wanted to take the kid's money. The huckster said to the boy, "You tell me a riddle. If I can't solve it, I'll pay you ten dollars. I'll tell you a riddle, and if you can't solve it then you pay me one dollar."

The boy knew he was no match intellectually for the man, but he decided to take the challenge anyway. The potential of making ten bucks was too good to pass up.

So he hit the man with a riddle. "What has one hundred legs, shouts from a steeple, but can't swim?"

The man was stumped. He agonized for half an hour until finally he gave up. He admitted, "I don't know," while he peeled off ten crisp one-dollar bills. "Eight, nine, ten . . . OK, now you have to tell me: What has one hundred legs, shouts from a steeple, but can't swim?"

The kid replied, "I have no idea; here's your dollar!"

Jesus spoke in riddles about this kingdom life, which is like a treasure hidden in a field, a pearl of great price; it's a deal too good to pass up—but many times we're just not receptive. We forget the part we must play in understanding. Our hearts are hard like a firm pathway where a seed cannot grow. Thus, we miss out on an opportunity of a lifetime.

2. Rocks. Some seeds fell on the rocks. Jesus offered this explanation: "The seed on the rocky soil represents those who hear the message and immediately receive it with joy. But since they don't have deep roots, they don't last long. They fall away as soon as they have problems or are persecuted for believing God's word" (verses 20, 21, NLT).

The people listening to Jesus could identify with shallow soil and stony ground. Still today, much of the land in Palestine is a foundation of rock covered by a thin layer of topsoil. While roots may start to sprout, there is no chance of growth. In using this word picture, Jesus taught that growth requires deep soil.

Richard Foster starts his book *Celebration of Discipline* by saying, "Superficiality is the curse of our age." It's a shallow world of hollow relationships, superficial conversations, hurried moments of prayer, too much screen time, and trivial commitments.

This superficiality is fueled by technology. CNN reports that

> the average American spends nearly half a day staring at a screen.
>
> A new Nielsen Company audience report reveals that adults in the United States devoted about 10 hours and 39 minutes each day

> to consuming media during the first quarter of this year. . . .
>
> "The overall results don't surprise me," said Steve Gortmaker, a professor of health sociology at Harvard University. . . .
>
> The report reveals a dramatic one-hour increase over last year in how often the average American adult gorges on media in a day. During the same time period last year, Nielsen reported that people spent about nine hours and 39 minutes engaging with gadgets.[4]

Professor of evolutionary psychology Robin Dunbar did a study to answer the question, Does the size of your social media network have any correlation to having more friends in real life? Here's the conclusion of his study: "We might have 150 or 5,000 Facebook friends, but our true relationship with the majority of these people is essentially insignificant."[5]

Relationally, mentally, and spiritually, most people prefer Jet Skis to scuba diving. Skimming the surface, racing at Mach speeds rather than going deep—relating with God and others in deeply significant ways, reading great authors that challenge us to think profoundly—we don't want scuba diving; we want Jet Skis.

Jesus says some seed falls on rocky soil—that is, people hear the message and get all excited but then when problems arise they bail—change jobs, change marriage partners, change ministries, change small groups, change churches. Roots require time, toughness, and perseverance.

So how deep are your roots? Are you tearing through life and relationships and work and church on a Jet Ski? Or are you scuba diving? Are you going deep and really meeting the challenges of life?

3. Thorns. The third type of soil is filled with thorns and weeds. On this one, Jesus offers this explanation: "The seed that fell among the thorns represents those who hear God's word, but all too quickly the message is crowded out by the worries of this life and the lure of wealth, so no fruit is produced" (verse 22, NLT).

This part of the story involves soil that's soft enough and deep enough to sustain growth. The problem is clutter. There is soil, but the nutrients are being wasted on weeds.

Perhaps this is the most dangerous soil condition of all, because it's so subtle. Our lives are not necessarily cluttered with bad things. In this condition, you may say, "My heart is not hard toward God. I'm not defiant or rebellious or deliberately superficial. I'm not the kind of person who bounces around from thing to thing. I've been involved in the same community, same church, same ministry for a long time. My life is just cluttered."

It's like a religious edition of the reality show *Hoarders*. This hit series captures the true stories of people with a compulsion for clutter. On the show, loved ones, psychologists, and organizational experts are brought in to try to help hoarders clear out the clutter.

You may ask, Why would anyone choose to live that way? I don't get it either. Pastor Clark Cothern observes,

> Most people who watch this show have the same reaction: they can't believe that people just won't let go of all the stuff that's slowly sabotaging important relationships and harming themselves. Unfortunately, most viewers don't see that at times all of us can act like hoarders when it comes to our spiritual lives. For instance, I have a tendency to misplace my affections; to value some things more highly than I ought, to cling to some things that aren't doing me any good—like worry, resentment, gossip, pride, self-righteousness, lust, or anger. The truth is, most of us may not clutter our lives with physical stuff, but we're just as guilty of emotional or spiritual hoarding.[6]

We all have our weeds, don't we?

Jesus warns of this deadly enemy. It can choke your spiritual vitality. It can drain you of purpose. It can make a mockery of your good intentions. It will choke off the spiritual life inside of you.

4. Good soil. But the story doesn't end there. Jesus goes on to explain that when the soil is soft and the dirt is deep and the ground is uncluttered, watch out! Growth is inevitable!

"But the seed falling on good soil refers to someone who hears the word and understands it. This is the one who produces a crop, yielding a hundred, sixty or thirty times what was sown" (verse 23).

Jesus would often use embellishment in order to describe the abundance, the richness of the kingdom of God. Such is the case in this story. The listeners would have been aware that at harvest, one seed would generally lead to one stalk and a head of grain. In a bad year, there might be but a couple of grains per stalk. In a good year, farmers would get twenty or even twenty-five grains per stalk.

But Jesus blows the ratios out of the field. He says the seed could yield thirty, sixty, or even one hundredfold! Such numbers were beyond believable. The point is that the fruitfulness that God desires for His people is beyond human comprehension or ability.

Clearly, Jesus wanted to encourage His followers. For we find ourselves in this story not just as the soil. We are also called to be sowers. We are given the privilege of sowing the seed.

Jesus knew this would present a tough test. So He tells us up front that most seed will fall on unproductive soil. "Nonetheless," He says, "don't despair. Don't quit. Keep planting seeds because the harvest is coming. And when that happens, watch out. The results will blow your mind!"

Remember this the next time you feel discouraged with the anemic results of your soul-winning efforts. Think about Jesus and the failure He experienced. He drew massive crowds, but most of them melted away. When He shared hard truth, John 6:66 says, "From this time many of his disciples turned back and no longer followed him."

The church leaders—who you would assume to be the most receptive to God's teaching—turned out to be bad soil. His disciples deserted Him. His family questioned Him. The Romans washed their hands of Him. The mob taunted Him.

As He anguished on the cross, you have to wonder if He wondered, *Did any of the seed take? Was it worth this sacrifice? Will there be any growth from the seeds I scattered?*

On the cross, Jesus is flanked by two thieves. Bad soil, both of them. No hope of seeds germinating in their stony hearts, right? One thief mocks Him. He asks, "Why don't You save Yourself and save us?" The other criminal asks, "Would You remember me?" Nobody would have guessed there was good soil in this guy. And yet, Jesus assures him of eternal life.

In His waning hours, Jesus plants still another seed, and then He dies. But He did not remain dead. For the grave could no more end His life than the soil can steal life from a seed.

Jesus understood that death begets life; hardship produces hope. "Unless a kernel of wheat falls to the ground and dies, it remains only a single seed," Jesus said. "But if it dies, it produces many seeds" (John 12:24).

Friend, don't be discouraged. Don't let the barren crops bump you off mission. And whatever you do, don't stop sowing seeds. For the Sower is at work. He promises that some seeds will take root in good soil. And the harvest He has in mind is beyond belief.

For reflection

1. "All healthy organisms grow." What does the growth (or lack of growth) suggest about the health of your church? If a church is not growing, what are some of the potential obstacles preventing growth?
2. "Church growth is a partnership between God and man. Churches grow by the power of God through the skilled effort of people" (Rick Warren). What specific efforts must we put forth in order to see the church grow?
3. Prayerfully assess the condition of your heart.

Hard	1	2	3	4	5	6	7	8	9	10	Pliable
Shallow	1	2	3	4	5	6	7	8	9	10	Deep
Cluttered	1	2	3	4	5	6	7	8	9	10	Clean

4. Discuss Richard Foster's observation that "superficiality is the curse of this age." Do you agree or disagree? Why or why not?
5. Ask God to help you get a vision for the wildly fruitful harvest He has in mind for you.
6. In John 4:36, Jesus says, "The one who reaps draws a wage and harvests a crop for eternal life, so that the sower and the reaper may be glad together." Notice that sowers and reapers will both draw a wage and "be glad together" as they see those they've witnessed to in heaven. Compare that verse to 1 Corinthians 9:25, where we are promised "a crown that will last forever" if we are faithful in sharing Jesus with others. How do these promises inform your intention to be a faithful witness for Jesus?
7. Where is God asking you to sow seed?

---

1. Jacob Sahms, "Modern Day Parables," February 19, 2013, https://mustardseedthoughts.com/2013/02/19/modern-day-parables-21713/.

2. Mark Maske, "Hard to Get a Grasp on Defensive Linemen," *Washington Post*, April 22, 2005, D14.

3. Rick Warren, *The Purpose Driven Church* (Grand Rapids, MI: Zondervan, 1995), 60.

4. Jacqueline Howard, "Americans Devote More Than 10 Hours a Day to Screen Time, and Growing," CNN, updated July 29, 2016, http://www.cnn.com/2016/06/30

/health/americans-screen-time-nielsen/index.html.

5. Chris Matyszczyk, "You Can Only Really Count on 4 of Your 150 Facebook Friends, Study Says," CNET.com, January 20, 2016, https://www.cnet.com/news/only-4-of-your-150-facebook-friends-are-actual-friends-says-study/.

6. Clark Cothern, in a sermon titled, "Wrestling With the Enemy," preached at Living Water Community Church, Ypsilanti, Michigan, quoted in "The TV Show 'Hoarders' Exposes Our Misplaced Affections," PreachingToday.com, accessed November 29, 2017, http://www.preachingtoday.com/illustrations/2011/august/1082211.html.

Chapter 10

MUSTARD AND YEAST

Matthew 13:31–33

The parables of the mustard seed and the yeast make the same point: the incredible contrast between the small beginnings of the kingdom and its epic expansion. In each case, it is a short tale with a sharp truth.

> "The kingdom of heaven is like a mustard seed, which a man took and planted in his field. Though it is the smallest of all seeds, yet when it grows, it is the largest of garden plants and becomes a tree, so that the birds come and perch in its branches."
>
> He told them still another parable: "The kingdom of heaven is like yeast that a woman took and mixed into about sixty pounds of flour until it worked all through the dough" (Matthew 13:31–33).

The mustard seed

First, let's consider the parable of the mustard seed. My love for mustard dates way back to when I was eight years old. Mom sent me across the street to Kmart to purchase a jar of mustard. Estimating the cost per ounce, even as a young boy I knew the biggest jar was the best buy.

When I proudly presented the purchase to Mom, she gasped. "Karl," she said, "what were you thinking? Why did you buy such a big container?"

This story is now a part of Haffner lore. The details vary—depending on who's telling the story. Mom maintains I bought a fifty-gallon drum.

I remember it being more like a gallon. In any case, she said, "We will *never*, in a million years, eat this much mustard!"

Here again, she was exaggerating. As I recall, we scraped the jar clean at my wedding reception.

To this day, I have a strong affection for mustard! The little seed was highly valued in the ancient world as well. Both the Greeks and Romans used it as more than just a condiment. Mustard was applied to scorpion stings. Hippocrates praised mustard paste as a miracle remedy capable of soothing all manner of pains. Roman physicians used it to ease toothaches.

William Barclay points out that Jesus used the mighty little mustard seed as a metaphor to teach two points. The first is obvious; the other point is more nuanced.

The obvious teaching is this: "The kingdom of heaven starts from the smallest beginnings, but no one knows where it will end."[1]

This is an important principle for us to think about as we focus on sharing Jesus. Remember this: "The everyday commission" only gets done when ordinary people like you and me introduce Jesus to others and then journey with them as we grow together in God's kingdom. So this parable reminds us that common folk can accomplish uncommon things. By God's power, everyday people will change the world.

A witness must begin with a single person—that is, one mustard seed. William Barclay tells the story of a group of international students discussing how the Christian gospel might be spread. They talked of propaganda, literature, evangelistic series, media ministry, and so on.

Then a girl from Africa spoke. " 'When we want to take Christianity to one of our villages,' she said, 'we don't send them books. We take a Christian family and send them to live in the village, and they make the village Christian by living there.' "

Barclay concludes: "In a group or society, or school or factory, or shop or office, again and again it is the witness of one individual which brings in Christianity. The one man or woman set on fire for Christ is the person who lights that fire in others."[2]

Something very small can grow into something very big. And that, my friends, is how God intends to save this world!

Perhaps you are one of the ten and a half million visitors to the website RedPaperClip.com. But it's more than just a website. It is a movie. It is a book. It is a true story that captures the big point of this parable.

Kyle MacDonald was stuck in a dead-end job when he determined that he would start with a red paper clip and trade on the internet until he ended up with a house. First, he traded the red paper clip for a fish-shaped pen. Next, he traded the pen for a doorknob. He traded the door-knob for a Coleman stove. He traded the Coleman stove for an electric generator. He traded the electric generator for a Budweiser sign and a keg of beer, which he then traded for a snowmobile. Exactly one year and fourteen trades later, MacDonald finally reached his goal: he exchanged a part in a Hollywood movie for a home in Saskatchewan, Canada.

Fame, fortune, a book, a movie, and a home—it all began with one red paper clip. Converts, megachurches, and a movement that transforms the world—it all begins with one small mustard seed. There's no question that Jesus was driving at this central point, but now consider the rest of the story.

Notice an important word that Jesus uses intentionally. Look again at verse 31 to see the subtler subtext. "The kingdom of heaven is like a mustard seed, which a man took and *planted* in his field" (emphasis added). We may think nothing of planting mustard seeds. But I assure you, when Jesus included that detail, listeners took note.

Vince Antonucci, in his book *Guerrilla Lovers: Changing the World With Revolutionary Compassion*, points out that a mustard seed grows like a weed. It will intertwine with other weeds, taking over the entire garden in short order. This helps you understand why Jewish law at the time of Jesus made it illegal to plant mustard seeds in a garden. Why? Because they knew it would grow and grow and grow. Soon, you'd have no other crops, only mustard.

So think about how people probably reacted when Jesus compared His kingdom to an illegal seed. Some were shocked: *Is He serious? Doesn't Jesus know about mustard?* Others giggled: *This Guy is hysterical. Imagine someone actually planting a mustard seed! LOL!* Others winced: *Jesus, hush! We like You. But if You insist on this crazy talk about Your kingdom, You'll get killed.*

Antonucci offers some modern-day equivalents:

> "What is the kingdom of God like? What shall I compare it to? It is like a vicious computer virus a man sent out in an email from his computer, and it spread and spread and infected more and more computers."

Or perhaps this: "What is the kingdom of God like? What shall I compare it to? It is like AIDS, which infected one person but soon spread and spread and became an epidemic as scores of people received it."

If we heard that, our heads would spin. We'd say, "What? Are you serious?" And the people who heard Jesus back then would have reacted the same way.[3]

So now with that understanding of the ancient world, you have to wonder: What was Jesus trying to teach us about the kingdom of God? Again, Antonucci is very insightful here. He writes,

I think Jesus is teaching us that the revolution is meant to be viral. It spreads like a disease. It's a disease you *want* to catch, but still it spreads like a disease. When you hang out with someone who has the flu, you catch the flu. Jesus is saying the revolution should be *sneezable*. The revolution should be contagious, and when it comes into an area, it should grow into an *epidemic*.

But it will only grow into an epidemic if it's done right. Weeds don't come in and announce they're taking over the garden. They don't invite all the other plants and vegetables to a meeting and ask them if they'd like to be taken over by the weeds. They don't hand out tracts explaining the benefits of a garden overrun by weeds. They don't wear weed T-shirts. They don't put a billboard up for all the vegetation to see: "For the Gardener so loved the garden, he gave his one and only weed."

No, a weed comes in unannounced, popping up very subtly, and it starts to grow. Then another weed pops up. And if these two weeds meet up, they'll get enmeshed, and then they'll intertwine with another weed. Soon they're pulling in flowers and plants, and eventually the entire garden is taken over by the weeds.

And Jesus teaches us that this is the way of his kingdom. The way his revolution is intended to function, the way it grows best, is not through public meetings, billboards, and TV. No, it's a love revolution that spreads person to person, one individual to another. And when we try to make it something it's not, it just won't work quite right. But when we live it out as it's supposed to be, watch out.[4]

Watch out is right.

"The little seed will become a tree," Ellen White tells us. "The last message of warning and mercy is to go to 'every nation and kindred and tongue' (Revelation 14:6-14), 'to take out of them a people for his name' (Acts 15:14; Revelation 18:1). And the earth shall be lightened with His glory."[5]

Yeast

As if for emphasis, Jesus goes on to another metaphor illustrating the same thing as the mustard seed. "The kingdom of heaven is like yeast that a woman took and mixed into about sixty pounds of flour until it worked all through the dough" (Matthew 13:33).

As in the previous story, Jesus used a shocking number here. You would assume the woman was making a loaf or two, but she used sixty pounds of flour. Add water and you're at more than one hundred pounds of dough. She's making enough bread to feed a football team! It's amazing—how such a massive amount of bread can be leavened by a little lump of yeast. Like the mustard seed, something so small will become something big—really big.

Here is another interesting detail: the word translated "mixed" is the same word meaning "to hide." In other words, the woman hides the leaven in the dough. That is how the kingdom works. There is something hidden about it. It doesn't happen as expected—it's unnoticeable at first, but unbelievable growth transpires. It starts with average, ordinary Janes and Joes—like you and me—as we blend into our world and interact with our neighbors and colleagues and families, and kingdom virtues get mixed into the world. And the world becomes transformed.

William Barclay spells it out:

> The whole point of the parable lies in one thing—*the transforming power of the leaven*. Leaven changed the character of a whole baking. Unleavened bread is like a water biscuit, hard, dry, unappetizing and uninteresting; bread baked with leaven is soft and porous and spongy, tasty and good to eat. The introduction of the leaven causes a transformation in the dough; and the coming of the kingdom causes a transformation in life.[6]

So what, exactly, causes this transformation? The *Huffington Post* explains how it works with yeast. Unlike baking soda or baking powder, yeast is a living organism in the same family as mushrooms. For yeast to effect the yummy transformation in bread, it needs four things. "When provided with water, food (in the form of sugar), warmth and some time, yeast makes our bread doughs rise by releasing carbon dioxide gas, which creates those tiny holes that make bread so light and airy."[7]

Provide four things, and you can't stop yeast from triggering a total transformation. Similarly, give Christ followers the same four things, and they will change the world. The gates of hell cannot thwart the advancement of God's kingdom.

1. Water. The first thing that yeast needs to be activated is water. Yeast will never work without water. Without water, there is no life.

Spiritually, the same principle rings true. Jesus said to the Samaritan woman at the well, "Everyone who drinks this water will be thirsty again, but whoever drinks the water I give them will never thirst. Indeed, the water I give them will become in them a spring of water welling up to eternal life" (John 4:13, 14).

Without Jesus, the Living Water, you will die. With Jesus, you will receive eternal life. It's that simple. We need Jesus.

So if you want to be a high-impact player for the kingdom of God, it is essential to drink daily of the Living Water. You must spend time getting to know Jesus. We can talk about sharing Jesus and growing His church—but if we are not drinking from the spring of Living Water each day, then our noblest efforts will be in vain. We will die.

2. Food. The second requirement for yeast to be activated is food. For yeast, this comes in the form of sugar (as is the case with too much of the food I eat!).

Jesus used this same metaphor when He said, "I am the bread of life. Whoever comes to me will never go hungry, and whoever believes in me will never be thirsty" (John 6:35).

For yeast to do its thing, it must have food and water. Jesus says, "To survive spiritually, you must have the Living Water and the Bread of Life." This is the only way transformation happens.

Pastor Morrie Venden used to tell of his desire in eighth grade to grow six feet tall. So he carefully measured his height and then went to the clothesline to hang on it as long as he could. Racing back to the measuring stick, he was very disappointed to discover that he had failed to grow.

Morrie concluded: "You don't grow by trying hard to grow; you grow by eating. If I had spent all of my time hanging on the clothesline post so I had no time to come in for dinner, it would have been safe to say that I would never have reached six feet tall, only six feet under."

Leaven doesn't try hard to make bread rise. If it's getting what it needs in food and water, the growth in bread inevitably happens. Likewise, we don't grow individually or as a church by focusing on growth. It only happens as we partake of the Living Water and the Bread of Life. Remain in close fellowship with Jesus, and the growth will follow.

3. Heat. The third essential ingredient that yeast needs is heat. As much as we resist it, heat is necessary for growth. We need trials and stress and disappointments. Hardship helps us grow.

"Too much comfort is dangerous. Literally. Researchers at the University of California at Berkeley did an experiment some time ago that involved introducing an amoeba into a perfectly stress-free environment. Ideal temperature, optimal concentration of moisture, constant food supply—the amoeba had an environment to which it had to make no adjustment whatsoever." So you would guess that the little amoeba would be delirious with delight, right? After all, "whatever it is that gives amoebas ulcers and high blood pressure was gone."

"Yet, oddly enough, it died. Apparently there is something about all living creatures, even amoebas, that demands challenge." We require heat the way we require food and water. "Comfort alone will kill us."[8] So it is, if our witness is to have maximum impact, we need to survive heat; we need hardship. Of course, we don't like this, but it's true. In survey after survey, when Christians are asked when their faith matured the most, the top answer is always, "During times of hardship and struggle." Why is this? Well, it's because hope is born out of heat. Paul puts it like this: "We boast in the hope of the glory of God. Not only so, but we also glory in our sufferings, because we know that suffering produces perseverance; perseverance, character; and character, hope" (Romans 5:2–4).

4. Time. For yeast to be activated, one final thing is needed: time. Right now, you may feel discouraged by the lack of growth in your life and your church. Trust God's timing. Your job is to drink of the Living Water, feast on the Bread of Life, trust God in the seasons of setbacks, and keep believing that "he who began a good work in you will carry it on to completion" (Philippians 1:6).

Hang on through the heat! Give it time. For God is good, and He has everything under control. Someday, time will catch up with God's goodness. Until that day, remain faithful in fulfilling "the everyday commission."

"The study of evangelism starts with the assumption that God is active, and that our efforts are only to participate in what God is already doing," says Mark Teasdale, associate professor of evangelism at Garrett-Evangelical Theological Seminary. "Our job is not to generate a mission, but to look to God through Jesus Christ in the power of the Holy Spirit, expecting miraculous power to burst forth as God moves to accomplish God's purpose—the redemption of all creation!"[9] For the mustard seed to grow and for the yeast to work, you need time. So for the time being, bloom where God has planted you and trust Him with the results.

Paul Borthwick gives us a picture of what this looks like in real life. He tells of running into Peter, one of his church members, working behind the counter at McDonald's. Knowing that Peter had graduated from Harvard University with a master's degree, he asked, "What are you doing here?"

"Well," Peter said, "I graduated in May, but I went four months without finding a job, so I said to myself, 'I need some income to pay bills.' So this is where I've ended up—at least for now."

"Sorry to hear that. It must be hard . . ."

"No!" Peter interrupted. "Don't be sorry. God has me here. This place is giving me awesome opportunities to share my faith. I'm on a shift that includes a Buddhist guy from Sri Lanka, a Muslim fellow from Lebanon, a Hindu lady from India, and a fellow Christian from El Salvador. It's awesome. I get to be a global missionary to my coworkers while asking 'would you like fries with that?' "[10]

For reflection

1. Read the parables of the mustard and yeast. How are they similar? How are they different? Why do you suppose Jesus told these two stories back-to-back?
2. Discuss the pros and cons of the two different approaches to evangelism. On the one hand, there is the public approach that seeks to attract the masses through television, public evangelistic meetings, and so on. On the other hand, there is the personal approach that focuses on the one-on-one conversations that carry through with discipleship over the long term. In your opinion, which approach is more effective? Are both approaches equally valid? Might a combination of the two work best? Why or why not?
3. Have you ever thought of the kingdom of God as a computer virus or AIDS? How does this comparison color your understanding of the story of the mustard seed?
4. Discuss the following statement in your small group: "We can talk about sharing Jesus and growing His church—but if we are not drinking from the spring of Living Water each day then our noblest efforts will be in vain. We will die."
5. When you think about the essential necessity of the Bread of Life to a Christian's spiritual well-being, what role does the church play? Does the pastor's weekly sermon supply enough Bread to sustain a healthy spiritual life? Is one meal per week enough for health and flourishing? Or is it the pastor's role to provide the recipe so you can make Bread at home in your daily walk with Jesus? What happens when Christians get hungry? Might they get grouchy and start cannibalizing one another if they are not being fed at home during the week? Whose responsibility is it to make certain that you are receiving a healthy spiritual diet of Living Water and the Bread of Life?
6. Share of a time in your spiritual journey when you felt "heat." In retrospect, did this experience result in spiritual growth? If so, in what way? What did God teach you in this season of heat?
7. How can you bloom where God has planted you? Do you ever want to rush God's timing? If so, what has God taught you about waiting on Him?

1. William Barclay, *The New Daily Study Bible: The Gospel of Matthew*, vol. 2, revised and updated (Edinburgh: Saint Andrew Press, 2001), 89.

2. Barclay, *The Gospel of Matthew*, 90.

3. Vince Antonucci, *Guerrilla Lovers: Changing the World With Revolutionary Compassion* (Grand Rapids, MI: Baker Books, 2010), 45.

4. Antonucci, *Guerrilla Lovers*, 45, 46 (italics in the original).

5. Ellen G. White, *God's Amazing Grace* (Washington, DC: Review and Herald®, 1973), 17.

6. Barclay, *The Gospel of Matthew*, 93 (italics in the original).

7. "Baking Yeast: A Guide to the Different Types," Huffington Post, May 31, 2012, http://www.huffingtonpost.com/2012/05/30/baking-yeast-types_n_1555862.html.

8. John Ortberg, *If You Want to Walk on Water, You've Got to Get Out of the Boat* (Grand Rapids, MI: Zondervan, 2001), 47.

9. Mark Teasdale, "Mark R. Teasdale," accessed November 29, 2017, https://www.garrett.edu/academics/faculty/mark-r-teasdale.

10. Paul Borthwick, *Great Commission, Great Compassion: Following Jesus and Loving the World* (Downers Grove, IL: InterVarsity Press, 2015), 46.

Chapter 11

TREASURE AND PEARL

Matthew 13:44–46

If Jesus was telling the story today, perhaps it would go something like this: The kingdom of heaven is like a treasure chest with enough Poké-Coins to purchase unlimited Incense, Lucky Eggs, Lure Modules, and yes, even Master Balls. One day, a trainer was wandering in a field when she stumbled upon the ultimate Pokémon prize. Her discovery would rack up XPs and catapult her to the 100th level. To prevent other trainers from finding the jackpot, she quickly plastered the property with "No Trespassing" signs and warnings that "Violators will be prosecuted to the full extent of the law."

The woman was ecstatic! This discovery meant that she would achieve the pinnacle of Pokémon glory—a heady space known only by the creator of Pokémon Go.

The trainer raced home and sold everything she owned—the beach condo, the Corvette convertible, and her prized original Macintosh computer that was built and signed by Woz and Steve Jobs.

Giddy with glee, the trainer then tracked down the owner and paid twice the appraised value of the land.

"But why are you so desperate for the property?" the owner asked.

"Well," she said, "let's just say I collect exotic insects and your field is bug heaven."

Here's the actual story: "The kingdom of heaven is like treasure hidden in a field. When a man found it, he hid it again, and then in his joy went and sold all he had and bought that field" (Matthew 13:44).

Typically, with parables, Jesus was making one primary point. Here, the main focus is the inestimable value of the treasure. When the man discovers it, he must secure it. He will do anything. He will stop at nothing. His obsession is possession of the treasure.

It's like the old story of the antique dealer who went to San Francisco. He visited an antique shop filled mostly with junk. He was about to leave when he noticed a cat drinking milk from a saucer. He knew it was from a rare set dating back to the Ming dynasty in China. Figuring it was worth far more than all his assets, he determined to secure the treasure.

He assumed the owner of the junk store had no idea of the saucer's value. So he schemed a plan. "You know," he said to the shop owner, "that's a remarkable cat that you have here. I'd really like to own that cat."

"Well, it's really not much of a cat," the owner said. "It's an ordinary cat and has no pedigree or anything, but it's our family cat. It's not for sale."

"Understood," the treasure hunter said, "but I'd really love to have the cat. It's a remarkable cat. I'll give you $250 for it."

"Well, it's a family cat. It's not really worth it, but if you want to pay $250 for it, OK."

"Great! Oh, and by the way, I need something to use to feed the cat. I'll throw in an extra ten bucks if you give me the saucer as well."

"Oh, I could never do that," the owner said. "That saucer is part of a rare set from the Ming dynasty, and its value is beyond price. But you know, ever since we started using it as a feeding dish, we've sold ten cats."

Jesus said this is how we are to understand the kingdom of God. It is like a treasure that is valuable beyond price. When people find it, the only sensible response is to do whatever it takes to possess it. Then He tells a very similar story with the same punchline. "Again, the kingdom of heaven is like a merchant looking for fine pearls. When he found one of great value, he went away and sold everything he had and bought it" (Matthew 13:45, 46).

Joachim Jeremias links these stories and explains,

> No price is too great to pay. The unreserved surrender of what is most valuable becomes a matter of course. The decisive thing in the

> twin parables is not what the two men give up, but their reason for doing so—the overwhelming experience of the splendor of his discovery. Thus it is with the kingdom of God. The effect of the joyful news is overpowering; it fills the heart with gladness; it changes the whole direction of one's life.[1]

From the outset of His public ministry, Jesus made it clear that the reason He came to earth was to share this good news. "The time has come," He said. "The kingdom of God has come near. Repent and believe the good news!" (Mark 1:15).

What is this "good news" that He came to share? That He asks us to share? "The kingdom of God has come near." The "good news" is simple: Jesus has come and now it is possible to know Him, to have a personal friendship with Him. So evangelism, then, is not convincing others to believe or behave like me. Evangelism is simply one friend telling another friend about a Friend. And this friendship changes everything.

Shortly after my wife, Cherié, and I started dating, she moved with her family back to Michigan. I wanted to be with her more than anything. Suddenly, I found myself in a deep funk doing nothing but obsessing about how much I desperately missed Cherié. Everything reminded me of her. I'd drive by a Baskin-Robbins and remember the date we had there. When I went by any park, I'd reminisce of the lazy afternoons we'd fly kites in the park. Whenever I saw a person who had a nose, I'd think, *Cherié has a nose. Man I miss her!*

I couldn't function. So I emptied out my savings account, borrowed some money from my parents, and hopped on a bus in Seattle and settled in for a long trip to Berrien Springs. I spent every penny I had because my desire to see her eclipsed every other longing in my heart.

When I finally arrived, I crawled inside a refrigerator box that was wrapped as a birthday present. When Cherié opened it, her jaw dropped in shock. I snapped a picture. Even her larynx is beautiful to me!

To what shall I compare the kingdom of God? It's like a heartsick college kid who spent everything he had to suffer for three days and three nights in the belly of a Greyhound to journey to the God-forsaken, mosquito-infested, pothole-riddled, humid, hot, smelly, and polluted shores of Lake Michigan just to be with the woman he loved.

To what shall I compare the kingdom of God? It's like the kid who spent every waking hour of her childhood going to the gym to perfect a floor routine and then treating the world to ninety seconds of choreographed precision and coming home with a gold medal.

To what shall I compare the kingdom of God? It's like buying a house and discovering a tree in the back that is ripe with the fruit of heaven—big, plump, luscious, carb-free, fat-free, peanut M&Ms.

To what shall I compare the kingdom of God? It is like a man named Jed, a poor mountaineer, who barely kept his family fed, then one day he was shootin' at some food, and up through the ground came a bubblin' crude. Oil that is, black gold, Texas tea. (And if you're connecting with that one, then you're as old as crude oil!)

To what can I compare the kingdom of God? Over and over, Jesus gives us pictures—earthy, pithy, common snapshots of what life in the kingdom of God looks like. Yeast, a mustard seed, a treasure, a pearl—all these metaphors help us to understand just how invaluable the kingdom of God really is.

You see, when we experience life down here as it is in heaven, we discover that anything we might give up down here pales in value to what we gain in a life with God. It's not like we make a sacrifice. What sane person wouldn't sell everything to secure a treasure that far eclipses the value of anything else they might possess? It's no sacrifice! It's just sanity! What else are you going to give your life to? If you've got something better, go give your life to that. No wonder Jesus labeled this message the "good news."

This is the gospel; this is the good news! The kingdom of God has come near, and it is possible to live in constant, intimate communion with Him. There is nothing that compares to the kingdom. Life with Jesus is good news.

A question

I have a question that has plagued me throughout my entire career: If the good news is so good, then why aren't our neighbors trampling down the doors of the church to get in? If this "treasure" is invaluable, and this "pearl" so precious, then why don't more people sell everything they have to secure the fortune? If the good news is so good, why does it feel as though we must resort to high-pressure sales techniques to find buyers?

Typically, good news is easy to sell. I remember an old episode of

Candid Camera. This was reality TV before they called it that. They would hide cameras to spy on people in staged situations. One time they recorded the reactions of people at a grocery store when they were at the checkout counter and told their purchases were free in honor of "Customer Appreciation Day." (Reality TV used to be a lot more wholesome before *The Bachelor* and the Kardashians came along!)

When people learned their groceries were free, how do you suppose they responded? They were not allowed to go get more groceries, but they could leave and tell others about it. Guess what? It didn't take long before everybody in town showed up. Such is the nature of good news. You can't keep it from going viral—it spreads naturally, inevitably, steadily. You can't stop good news from spreading.

So why is it so hard to spread the good news of the gospel? God offers eternal life for free, and yet most people aren't interested.

An answer

Pastor Morrie Venden would answer that it is because we tend to make religion more about rules than a relationship. So when we talk about "witnessing," we sometimes think this means we must convince others of "truth" (such as how the Sabbath is Saturday, not Sunday) rather than seeing evangelism as merely introducing people to Jesus.

In his book *The Life You've Always Wanted,* John Ortberg writes, "Groups have a tendency to be exclusive. Insiders want to separate themselves from outsiders. So they adopt boundary markers. These are highly visible, relatively superficial practices—matters of vocabulary or dress or style—whose purpose is to *distinguish* between those inside a group and those who are on the outside."[2]

In my faith tradition, we have boundary markers aplenty. Abstinence from tobacco, modest dress, Sabbath observance—these are ways you can tell if a person belongs to our religious tribe. Of course, there is nothing wrong with these lifestyle practices, but when they are held up as the criteria for entering into kingdom life, spirituality then becomes seriously flawed.

Perhaps that helps to explain why people are often repulsed by our good news. Dallas Willard writes, "How many people are radically and permanently repelled from [the way of Christ] by Christians who are unfeeling, stiff, unapproachable, boringly lifeless, obsessive, and dissatisfied?

Yet such Christians are everywhere, and what they are missing is the wholesome liveliness springing from a balanced vitality within the freedom of God's loving rule."[3]

"God's loving rule" is the kingdom of heaven. It is the buried treasure. It is the big pearl. It is that environment where God gets what God wants—namely, a personal friendship with you. Thus, sharing Jesus is not about talking people into joining our fraternity and getting them inside our boundary markers; rather, sharing Jesus is all about introducing them to a Friend. This is the good news: The kingdom of heaven has come in Jesus, and we can live in intimate friendship with Him.

When you understand this, it redefines faith, church, spirituality, religion, and especially evangelism.

This idea hit home last year when my laptop crashed and I lost all its data. When I got this news from the "genius" at the Apple store, I cried.

In trying to reconstruct my files from backups, I happened upon a file titled "Dad's rules for the dog." When we moved from Washington to Ohio, I told the girls they could get a dog—even though I never wanted one. But first, they had to agree to my rules. In this manifesto, I spelled out every conceivable scenario in which I might be inconvenienced by this mutt. "Dad will never exercise the dog. Dad will never feed the dog. Dad will never pet the dog. The fiduciary responsibilities of the dog rest solely upon our girls, Lindsey and Claire. On the day that the dog messes in the house or in the yard, thereupon on that day, the dog will surely die." You get the idea.

They got this Maltese-Poodle and named him Skipper. I wanted to name him "Repent" so I could go through the neighborhood calling, "Come, Repent . . ." (That way, I figured the little mutt would qualify as a tax deduction!)

No sooner did they bring this dog home than Skipper became my little buddy. We jogged hundreds of miles together. Whenever church members discarded me as a useless, inept, good-for-nothing pastor, I could always count on Skipper showing me unconditional love when I walked in the door at home. He fast became "Dad's dog." And Dad forgot all about his magnum opus of rules.

A couple years ago, Skipper got sick and went for several days without eating or drinking. As I was officiating at a wedding, my wife was taking him to the animal emergency room. She texted me with updates:

"Doesn't look good." "They're not sure what is wrong." "They may have to do surgery."

During the ceremony, I texted back, "I don't care what it costs, just keep Skip alive."

Good news: He survived!

But how did I go from "the fiduciary responsibilities of the dog rest solely upon our girls" to "I don't care what it costs . . ."? What changed?

Not to get weird here, and I know all illustrations fail on some level, but it really has to do with the relationship, doesn't it? I didn't title the document "Dad's rules for Skipper" because I didn't *know* Skipper. My rules were for "the dog." But through all those miles and meals and memories, everything changed.

Everything changes when the relationship replaces the rules. Evangelism becomes natural, unforced, and as easy as introducing your friends to your best Friend.

For reflection

1. Compare the stories of the treasure and the pearl. How are they similar? How are they different?
2. React to the statement, "Evangelism is not convincing others to believe or behave like me. Evangelism is simply one friend telling another friend about a Friend." How does this affect the way you think about personal evangelism? Does it make the practice of witnessing to others feel less intimidating or more? In what way?
3. Brainstorm with your small group about some earthy, pithy, common snapshots of what life in the kingdom of God looks like.
4. If the good news is so good, then why aren't our neighbors trampling down the doors of the church to get in? What are your thoughts?
5. What are the "boundary markers" in your church?
6. In matters of faith, do you tend to lean toward the "rules" or the "relationship" side of the spectrum? Is there a place for both in a person's spiritual walk? How do they interface together in the context of a local church?
7. How does the following quote tame the tension between rules and relationship? "All true obedience comes from the heart. It was heart work with Christ. And if we consent, He will so identify Himself with our thoughts and aims, so blend our hearts and minds into conformity to His will, that when obeying Him we shall be but carrying out our own impulses. The will, refined and sanctified, will find its highest delight in doing His service. When we know God as it is our privilege to know Him, our life will be a life of continual obedience."[4]

---

1. Joachim Jeremias, *The Parables of Jesus* (New York: Charles Scribner's Sons, 1970), 84, quoted in Brennan Manning, *The Relentless Tenderness of Jesus* (Grand Rapids, MI: Fleming H. Revell, 2004), 213.
2. John Ortberg, *The Life You've Always Wanted* (Grand Rapids, MI: Zondervan, 2002), 31.
3. Dallas Willard, *The Spirit of the Disciplines: Understanding How God Changes Lives* (New York: HarperCollins, 1988), 80.
4. White, *The Desire of Ages*, 668.

Chapter 12

DRAGNET AND HOMEOWNER

Matthew 13:47–52

Years ago, we were struggling in a church business meeting with issues surrounding a $1.5 million building project. One frustrated member captured the crowd with a simple yet graphic word picture. "How can we expect members to keep giving to this project when we don't know what we're doing?" Then he gave an illustration that hammered his point home. "We're asking our members to buy a car that doesn't have wheels."

That image stuck in the minds of many for months to come. It motivated us to clarify the details of the project before we launched the public campaign. The "car without wheels" word picture propelled us to action.

Repeatedly, in Matthew 13, Jesus gives us word pictures to describe the kingdom of God. "It is like the sower, the mustard seed, the leaven, the treasure, the pearl," He said. To conclude, He offers two more powerful word pictures.

> "Once again, the kingdom of heaven is like a net that was let down into the lake and caught all kinds of fish. When it was full, the fishermen pulled it up on the shore. Then they sat down and collected the good fish in baskets, but threw the bad away. This is how it will be at the end of the age. The angels will come and separate the wicked from the righteous and throw them into the blazing furnace, where there will be weeping and gnashing of teeth" (Matthew 13:47–50).

Being the master communicator that He is, Jesus used a word picture that connected well with fishermen. He says to them, "Notice how your daily work teaches you about the things of heaven."

In Bible days, fishermen used two different types of nets. One was a casting net. It was bell shaped and small enough to be managed by a single person. The other was a dragnet. Covering as much as a square mile of water surface, it was too unwieldly to be used by one fisherman. A group of guys would spread it out between two boats and then drag it toward the shoreline. Typically, it would be filled with all sorts of sea creatures, and maybe a tire or license plate, a dead camel—who knows?

Jesus describes the drill His fishing friends would have known well. When they pulled in the net, they separated the good fish from everything else. Keep in mind the Levitical guidelines for clean and unclean fish. Shellfish and bottom dwellers would be tossed into the unclean pile, and fish with fins and scales into the pile to keep.

Applying this to our day, William Barclay offers this commentary:

> There have always been two views of the Church—the exclusive and the inclusive. The exclusive view holds that the Church is for people who are good, people who are really and fully committed, people who are quite different from the world. There is an attraction in that view, but it is not the New Testament view. . . . It is not the place of any one of us to say who is committed to Christ and who is not. The inclusive view feels instinctively that the Church must be open to all, and that, like the dragnet, as long as it is a human institution it is bound to be a mixture. That is exactly what this parable teaches.[1]

Steve Bankes wanted to practice the "inclusive view" in his neighborhood. So he put a patio in his front yard. A *Chicago Tribune* article showed a picture of five adults relaxing on chairs, on a small patio under shade trees near a suburban street. A couple kids and a dog joined them as well. The reporter, Barbara Brotman, said, "It would have been charming, but unremarkable, if it had been in their backyard, the usual spot for patios. But this patio was in their front yard."

According to the article, the front-yard patio became like a friendship magnet for Mr. Bankes's neighbors, "especially when Steve had . . . set out a fire pit and built a bonfire. So people began to wander over, sit down and talk. It was so easy and low-key. No invitation required; if you saw people out there, you joined them." Steve called his patio "the Conversation Curve." He said his goal was "fishing for people." I'd say it's fishing for people with a dragnet, wouldn't you?

A year later, Brotman wrote a follow-up article. Apparently, Keith Speaks from Hammond, Indiana, read the story and called Bankes to discuss his "fishing for people" front-yard patio idea. Speaks works in community development, and he wanted to use the concept to foster friendships in his town. So Speaks started the "Please, Have a Seat!" program, which gives grants for homeowners to create "micro parks" in their front yards. The follow-up article described the unveiling ceremony for some of these micro parks: "Rev. Stephen Gibson, whose [church] has two benches of its own . . . gave a benediction. 'I ask God to bless this bench as a symbol of the spirit of welcome.' "[2] So let me challenge you to build a micro park in your front yard—cast a wide dragnet to include all people.

Myron Augsburger's commentary provides a succinct summary of this story. He writes, "The kingdom of heaven is as a net cast across the world, being pulled toward the final reckoning."[3]

Jesus provides a sobering snapshot of that final reckoning as He describes the wicked being thrown into the blazing furnace, "where there will be weeping and gnashing of teeth" (Matthew 13:50). Given the seriousness of the scene, it is no wonder that Jesus asks His followers, "Do you understand all these things?"

They said, "Yes, we understand" (verse 51, ERV).

Keep in mind that the biblical notion of "understanding" encompasses more than just a head knowledge. It has a very practical component. Jesus is challenging His disciples with the idea that it is not enough just to hear the seven parables He shared. Jesus wants His listeners to put them into practice. In Scripture, "understanding" includes both the head and the hands, knowing what to do, and then doing it.

It reminds me of the time that I bought a set of hair clippers, because when you sport my hairstyle, you really don't need to spend a lot of money at the salon. So I asked my daughter, Claire, "Do you think you could cut my hair?"

"Of course," she said. "It will only be five bucks."

Seemed fair, so I got everything ready . . . but Claire was nowhere to be found. She was holed up in my office, watching a YouTube video titled "How to Cut a Bald Man's Hair." She was acquiring head knowledge—which would then be put into practice with her hands.

Understanding includes both the head and the hands. As Jesus concludes His sermon, He wants to be certain the disciples understand His teaching by putting the parables into practice. This is the same way He concluded the Sermon on the Mount, when He said, "Therefore everyone who hears these words of mine and puts them into practice is like a wise man who built his house on the rock" (Matthew 7:24). Jesus then puts an exclamation point on the sermon with one final parable. So here in Matthew 13, Jesus asks them, "Do you understand?" and then He shares a final parable.

"Therefore every teacher of the law who has become a disciple in the kingdom of heaven is like the owner of a house who brings out of his storeroom new treasures as well as old" (Matthew 13:52). Bible.org offers this overview: "If the last parable is about the responsibility of evangelism, then this one is about the responsibility of edification. Edification is 'building others up.' How does edification relate to the Kingdom? Once someone is in the kingdom (the parable of the dragnet) they need to be taught."[4] This is "the everyday commission"—evangelism and edification. Every person who follows Jesus is uniquely qualified to reach and teach others because this person brings out of his or her storehouse "new treasures as well as old."

In referencing the "old," Jesus is complimenting the exceptional education and heritage of the disciples. But now that they know Jesus and have learned from Him, they are armed with "new treasures." So the knowledge of God's kingdom that they possessed before is newly illuminated by being with Jesus.

This is the kingdom of heaven: to live in relationship with Jesus. This is the homeowner who retrieves new treasures from the storeroom, for the ultimate treasure is Jesus Himself.

As Pastor Ken Mckinley puts it:

> That treasure is Jesus Christ! It's Christ! His person, His work, His Word, His blood, His cross, His empty tomb, His reign at the Father's right hand. It's knowing Him and being known by Him! That's the treasure! And when Matthew says, we pull out both old and new he's referring to the Old Covenant Scriptures that speak

> of Christ and promise His coming . . . and the new [which] is the New Covenant Scriptures that talk about when He came, and what He has done, and what He continues to do within His Church. They talk about how Jesus fulfilled all those Old Covenant promises. Understand—all Scripture is about Christ![5]

It's all about Christ. Both the "reaching" and "teaching" components of "the everyday commission" must always, only, be all about Christ. In his book *Evangelism for the Rest of Us*, Mike Bechtle tells of the time their miniature schnauzer named Gretchen disappeared in the backyard of a friend's house. After hours of searching and panic, they found her, stuck under a spa. Only after hearing the whimpering did they realize that one of the redwood boards on the frame was loose. Gretchen had crawled inside through the open slat, but then the board had dropped back into place, trapping the scared dog.

Bechtle writes,

> I could see her, but she couldn't see me. I was shining the light directly into her eyes, and she couldn't see which way to move. So I turned the flashlight around and shone it in my own face so she could see me. Immediately she rushed through that open slat and into my arms.
>
> That's one way to picture evangelism. Too often we think we need to shine the gospel on people's shortcomings and sins so it will be obvious where the problem is. But that's not our job. Through our lives, our words, and our relationships, we should be shining the light so they get a clear, accurate view of Christ. That's where they'll find the exit from the pain in their life. Jesus said, "I, when I am lifted up from the earth, will draw all men to myself" (John 12:32). We simply need to lead people to the Savior, not drag them or force them.[6]

This is our mission: Lift up Jesus. We must stay close to Jesus for everything we need in order to be effective witnesses for Him. Then, of course, we must stay close to unbelievers for opportunities to share Jesus. And finally, we must stay close to believers so we can encourage one another in Jesus.

For reflection

1. Do you tend to embrace an "exclusive" (keep the good people in and the bad people out) view or an "inclusive" (all people—good *and* bad are welcome) view of the church? Share your rationale. In your mind, is this a "right" or "wrong" answer? Explain.
2. Brainstorm ways you could turn your front yard into a micro park. (You may have to think metaphorically here!)
3. Jesus described a day of judgment where there will be "weeping and gnashing of teeth." When leading people to Christ, how much ought we to talk about this sobering reality? Is there a way to frame "the judgment" so that it is good news? If so, how?
4. How can you use your head and your hands in sharing your faith? How do you accomplish both evangelism and edification in fulfilling Christ's commission to reach and teach lost people? How do you make all of it Christ-centered?
5. List practical ways to "lift up Jesus" in everything you think, say, and do.
6. After sharing several parables in Matthew 13, Jesus asked His disciples the question, "Do you understand?" How would you answer His question? Keep in mind the biblical idea of all that "understanding" entails.
7. So now, what is your game plan to fulfill "the everyday commission"?

---

1. Barclay, *The Gospel of Matthew*, 105.
2. Barbara Brotman, "Front Patio Makes a Great Hook if Fishing for People," *Chicago Tribune* August 3, 2009; Barbara Brotman, "Oak Park Neighbors' Spot Has East Chicago Talking," *Chicago Tribune*, August 9, 2010.
3. Myron S. Augsburger, *Matthew*, The Preacher's Commentary, vol. 24 (Nashville, TN: Thomas Nelson, 1982), 169.
4. "2. The Parables of Matthew 13," Bible.org, accessed November 30, 2017, https://bible.org/seriespage/2-parables-matthew-13.
5. Ken Mckinley, "Trained for the Kingdom," May 29, 2014, http://www.sermoncentral.com/sermons/trained-for-the-kingdom-ken-mckinley-sermon-on-training-disciples-185637?page=3.
6. Bechtle, *Evangelism for the Rest of Us*, 152, 153.

POSTSCRIPT

In his book *I Became a Christian and All I Got Was This Lousy T-Shirt*, Vince Antonucci tells of taking a day for fasting and prayer at Burger King (fasting from food, that is, not Coke ☺). Two minutes into his time of solitude, a "dirty, smelly guy" started pacing in front of his table. Unable to ignore him, Vince asked if he could be of help.

The guy was from India and barely spoke English. And yes, he needed help filling out a job application to work at the fast food joint. A frustrating hour later, the paperwork was done and Vince thought, *Good, glad that's over. Now to get to my solitude stuff.*

Two minutes later, the guy returned to Vince's table. *Now what?* Vince wondered. "Are you hungry? Can I order you a meal?" The guy said "yes" and "yes." So Vince forked over a few bucks for a burger and some fries.

"The guy appreciated it," Vince recalls. "He really appreciated it. He grabbed both my hands and started rubbing them all over his face and neck. I thought, *Oh . . . my . . . goodness! This is so weird!* Finally, after the thirty most awkward seconds of my life, he grabbed my money and disappeared. I thought, *Wow. Well, it's a good thing that I helped him. But I am so glad that's over.* I went back to reading."

Of course, the guy returned to the table, obviously wanting to talk to his new friend. Soon, the open Bible on the table came up in the conversation. Vince explained that he was a Jesus follower. On cue, the guy pulled out a picture of Jesus. "Yeah," Vince said, "that's who I'm telling you about!" Then the guy pulled out pictures of Buddha, Muhammad, a goat, Reggie Jackson, Regis Philbin, the Dalai Lama, and Bea Arthur. He became very serious and asked, "Do you know what God's name is?"

Vince said, "I believe his name is Jesus. Jesus is God's Son."

"No!" the guy said, "God's name is twenty-one!"—referring to twenty-one different names for God in various world religions.

But then he asked Vince, "Do you know who is God today?"

Vince writes,

> I answered, "Twenty-one?"
>
> "No," he said. "Today, you are God to me."
>
> "No, I'm not God," I responded.
>
> "Yes, you are," he countered.
>
> "No," I explained. "I'm trying to show you the love of God, but I'm not God."
>
> "No. Today you love me," he said. "You help me. You feed me. Who is God? He loves, he helps, he feeds. Today, you are God to me."
>
> In one sense he was theologically wrong, because I'm certainly not God. But in another sense, he was right. Because God *has* asked me to represent him, to be his ambassador.
>
> We need to *be* the good news before we share the good news so that our gospel has integrity.[1]

So true, isn't it? Before we invite others into this kingdom way of life, we must experience it for ourselves. Otherwise, our witness has zero credibility.

I think of the story about Major Gennady Osipovich, a USSR air force pilot. He had volunteered to give a talk about peace at the school where his children attended. In order to get time off during the day to give his talk, he had signed up for night duty. That's how Major Osipovich found himself patrolling the skies over the eastern regions of the Soviet Union on September 1, 1983—the night Korean Air Lines Flight KE007 strayed into Soviet airspace.

Soon Major Osipovich was caught in a series of blunders and miscommunication. In the end, he followed orders and shot down the unidentified aircraft. In other words, it was this same air force major preparing to talk about peace that plunged 269 passengers and crew to their deaths, thus triggering an international incident that pushed world powers to a standoff.

Our talk is important. However, our actions carry far more weight. Therefore, we must model our lives in Christ. As we do, we participate in the blessings of kingdom life—which then makes us all the more effective in evangelism.

"Those who impart to others of the riches of the grace of heaven, will be themselves enriched," Ellen White tells us. "The ministering angels are waiting, longing, for channels through which they can communicate the treasures of heaven. . . . We cannot diminish our treasure by sharing it. The more we enlighten others, the brighter our light will shine."[2]

So let your light shine.

Some years ago, I saw a beautiful picture of God's light shining through His people. When we landed in Guam, I felt like I'd been dragged through a carwash of Brillo pads drenched in battery acid. Every part of my body ached (including the skin on my elbow where Tubba—a buddy of mine in fifth grade—said humans have no feeling). A high fever, swollen throat, itchy eyes, and news of another Boston Red Sox loss all contributed to my misery.

For nine months, I had anxiously anticipated speaking at this camp meeting, but when the plane landed, all I wanted was to sleep until the Second Coming. Nevertheless, since the local conference covered all expenses, I felt obliged to grease up the throat with drugs and eke out a sermon that evening.

The following day I was scheduled to preach four times. That task felt as likely as the Cleveland Browns winning the Super Bowl. Still, I smiled when Pastor Nambu arrived early to escort me to the campgrounds.

"You feeling any better this morning?" he asked.

"No," I said. "I feel like I have sandpaper lodged in my throat."

"I'm sorry."

I rested my head against the car window and closed my eyes. As we maneuvered the twists up a mountain road, we curved around a corner and nearly crashed into a stranded motorist parked in the lane. Her old Ford Escort hissed like Old Faithful.

Pastor Nambu pulled over to offer the woman some assistance. When he stopped, I confess my thoughts were not Christian. *We don't have time for this. Let's just get to camp meeting so I can preach my sermons.* (Never mind that my sermons were all on the topic of how we are called to show the love of Jesus to people in need!) *Let me get this day over with so I can go back to bed.*

"Can we push your car off the road so you don't get hit?" Pastor Nambu asked the woman.

"Sure," she said, "but there isn't much of a shoulder here."

"I know, but you're on a blind corner and I'm afraid someone might hit you."

Reluctantly, I joined them and pushed the car to a safer spot. Just then, another car stopped to help. I recognized the driver as an Adventist from the night before.

"Can we give you a tow?"

"No," she said. "I called my husband, and he's got a tow truck coming. Getting me this far off the road has been very helpful."

As I turned toward our car, the lady surprised me with a question. "Are all of you Seventh-day Adventists?"

"Yes!" I said. "Are you an Adventist?"

"No," she said, "I'm not, but I can see you're dressed like you're going to church. Besides, I've been to the Adventist clinic and find the people there to be the nicest folk on the island. When you stopped to help, I reckoned you were from that clinic."

I smiled and wished her well. Then she added, "If I were to ever join a church, it would be with the Adventists because they're always helping people in need. God bless you!"

Jesus once said, "By this will all people know that you are genuine Seventh-day Adventist Christians—that you love one another" (John 13:35; my paraphrase).

So be a witness for Jesus. How? Live God's love.

---

1. Vince Antonucci, *I Became a Christian and All I Got Was This Lousy T-Shirt* (Grand Rapids, MI: Baker Books, 2008), 179–181. Barclay, The New Daily Study Bible: The Gospel of Matthew,

2. Ellen G. White, "Receiving to Impart," *Review and Herald*, April 4, 1907, par. 9.